NEIGHBOURHOOD RENEWAL

CASE STUDIES & CONVERSATIONS

FOCUSING ON ADULT & COMMUNITY LEARNING

LENFORD WHITE

Published by the Department for Education and Skills
and the National Institute of Adult Continuing Education (England and Wales)

DfES
Moorfoot
Sheffield
S1 4PQ

NIACE
21 De Montfort Street
Leicester
LE1 7GE
Company registration number 2603322
Charity registration number 1002775

First published 2002

department for
education and skills

ⓝiace

NIACE has a broad remit to advance the interests of adult learners. Ii works with national and local government, education providers, employers, the voluntary sector and others to promote equal opportunities of access to learning for all adults.

Cataloguing in Publication Data
A CIP record of this title is available from the British Library

ISBN 1 86201 170 2

Designed and typeset by Lee Robinson / Ad Lib Design, London
Printed and bound in Great Britain by Alden Press, Oxford
Cover photo: *Chloe Douglas, London and Quadrant Housing*

NEIGHBOURHOOD RENEWAL
CASE STUDIES & CONVERSATIONS

FOCUSING ON ADULT &
COMMUNITY LEARNING

Contents

Introduction

The Prime Minister lauched *New Commitment to Neighbourhood Renewal – A National Strategy Action Plan* on 15 January 2001. The Strategy sets out the Government's vision for narrowing the gap between deprived neighbourhoods and the rest of the country, so that "within 10 to 20 years, no one should be seriously disadvantaged by where they live". This new commitment has been made in the light of sustained research by the Social Exclusion Unit culminating in its report *Bringing people together: a national strategy for neighbourhood renewal* (1998) and the follow-up work carried out by 18 Policy Action Teams (PATs) in a range of areas including housing, education, crime and health.

The PATs, made up of government officials, academics and residents, put forward 569 recommendations, of which 85 per cent were accepted and incorporated into the national strategy action plan for neighbourhood renewal.

WHAT IS NEIGHBOURHOOD RENEWAL?

Neighbourhood renewal is about taking a strategic approach in order to improve the quality of life for people who live in the poorest communities in Britain. It is also about recognising that residents in hundreds of poor neighbourhoods see their basic quality of life increasingly detached from the majority of people in this country. What has led to this increased detachment in Britain, one of the richest countries in the world? According to the national strategy action plan, it is the result of

> **a complex combination of factors. Some of the factors are social and economic changes that have affected many countries. When these combine they can create a complex and fast moving vicious cycle.**

Factors such as mass joblessness because of recession, family breakdown and reliance on benefits, declining popularity of social housing and an increasing concentration of vulnerable people in deprived neighbourhoods all contribute towards poverty. Failure to address these problems adequately at both national and local government levels has compounded problems because, until now, lessons from previous regeneration initiatives have not always been learned.

This is particularly true in ensuring genuine community participation in decision-making. The national strategy recognises that 'neighbourhood renewal starts from a proper understanding of the needs of communities' and that the most effective interventions are often those where communities are actively involved in their design and development. This includes communities of interest, such as people who are black or from minority groups, as well as geographically defined communities.

LEARNING AND NEIGHBOURHOOD RENEWAL

The main focus of the case studies presented in this book is on adult learning in a community context: adult and community learning (ACL). This recognises the fact that, without adult learning, the national strategy for neighbourhood renewal will not work. It should be recognised, however, as it is in the report from Policy Action Team 16: Learning Lessons (March 2000), that learning and the acquisition of new skills and knowledge flow in several directions to be channelled and harnessed by residents, local government workers, civil servants and all partners involved in neighbourhood renewal. With regard to local government workers, the report notes that:

> **Hard-pressed public sector professionals and practitioners do not, by and large, receive the support and training they need to work effectively in disadvantaged neighbourhoods. This may be because they receive no training, or because the training they receive is of a poor quality.**

Although ACL has a variety of definitions and meanings, in essence it is about flexible learning, provided (often for non-traditional learners) in places that are appropriate, at times that are convenient, in a format and with a content that is meaningful and by teachers who are relevant. Typically, the relevant teacher has an empathy and understanding of the learners that he or she is teaching and ideally comes from the same community as the learner.

ACL has a strong focus on widening participation and on the delivery of 'first-rung' provision; it stresses learner-centred provision and occurs in contexts that are not always explicitly educational. These contexts are illustrated throughout the case studies. Invaluable skills are acquired by learners who support each other in local community organisations and campaign in support of communities of interest.

THE MAIN PURPOSE OF THE BOOK

This book has several purposes. First, it supports the National Institute of Adult Continuing Education (NIACE)'s pack for Local Education Authorities, *Learning for the future: neighbourhood renewal through adult and community learning*. The pack explores issues such as partnerships, accessing resources, target-setting and quality improvement. It is a 'how-to-do-it' guide for those involved in adult learning activities in local government. This book is the pack's supportive arm and illustrates how neighbourhood renewal is being conducted in practice. Its readership is the same as for the pack, but it has broader implications for anyone involved in neighbourhood renewal, local government, colleges, community groups, Councils for Voluntary Service and other voluntary sector organisations.

This book is also aimed at statutory bodies such as the Department for Education and Skills (DfES), the book's sponsors, the Learning and Skills Council (LSC), the Local Government Association (LGA), government offices for the regions and the Department of Transport, Local Government and the Regions (DTLR). It is relevant as a learning tool, enabling learning from knowledge about what does and does not work.

The book is also about sharing good practice, in recognition that those involved in regeneration initiatives (and all of them involve adult learning) will be facing the same issues. If an innovative outreach project has worked in Grantham, then let's have a look at it and see if it can be modified and reapplied in Morpeth. After all, it's not always necessary to go through a painful process in order to appreciate what develops out of it. If someone has something that works, take it and apply it: there will be plenty of other painful experiences to learn from in the future, as neighbourhood renewal is a learning experience for all of us and is bound to throw up constant challenges calling for new ways of doing things.

DEPRIVED COMMUNITIES

The case studies presented in this book cover a range of geographical areas, not all of which fall within the nation's 88 most deprived districts, although a significant proportion do. These include the North East, the North West and London.

In some places in Britain, 40 per cent of residents rely on means-tested benefits, 75 per cent of young people fail to get five GCSEs at grades A* – C and homes are impossible to fill, because those who can get out do so, leaving behind the least socially mobile.

These neighbourhoods exist right across the country, north and south, rural and urban. They may be cut off on the edge of cities, or close to city centres and wealthy suburbs. They may be high-rise council estates, or streets of private rented or even owner-occupied homes. (Neighbourhood Renewal Strategy, 2001)

A mountainous portfolio of regeneration and urban development initiatives has been built up in the poorest parts of Britain, often in urban areas, and they have not always worked. In order to prevent this mountain growing, logic suggests that we should share our experiences in the area of neighbourhood renewal early, celebrating successes, but at the same time warning our partners of traps, pitfalls and unfruitful lines of investigation.

The drawing together of a number of case studies that focus on the role of education in regeneration is particularly relevant, primarily because education is an obvious vehicle through which to demonstrate that something has changed. This is true, whether it be a black young adult acquiring the skills to participate more effectively in a local residents' association, or the preparation for and successful employment of residents in New Deal for Communities areas, or the provision of tailor-made training opportunities in new industries

Through various education initiatives it is possible to assess were learners 'are at' from the outset and, after various interventions, to show where they end up.

GENUINELY EMPOWERING PEOPLE

Neighbourhood renewal is all about learning, and in some cases very hard lessons have had to be learned in relation to making decisions and shifting the balance of power. The real tests of 'community capacity-building' initiatives, for example, are in being brave enough to let someone else take hold of the reins and in playing a supportive and empathetic role, particularly when that someone steers off course or is critical about standard procedures and modes of operation.

The learning dimension of neighbourhood renewal, according to various neighbourhood renewal strategies, involves putting the poorest in our society in the driving seat. This is acknowledgment that people who live in poor areas know their neighbourhoods best. They are aware of the issues in their neighbourhoods and will be well placed to know how to address these and to identify who should take the lead on developments. As the report of Policy Action Team 16: Learning Lessons recognises,

> **Neighbourhood renewal cannot be successful without the active involvement of the community. Yet community leaders and their organisations do not always receive sufficient funding, support and training to play and effective role.**

This sensible acknowledgement of the strategic role of local residents in neighbourhood renewal is reflected in a number of projects featured in this book, such as the Community Leadership Project being piloted through the Bernie Grant Trust. This project relies on local residents to identify those who are best able to take the lead on community-based developments and represent 'the community' in strategic discussions with various public sector bodies and their employees, including the police, local government workers and civil servants.

It can be difficult for public sector bodies to share power with local residents and community-based organisations; this power-sharing also presents challenges to mainstream organisations not used to working in partnership. Learning can be difficult when what is being presented breaks from tradition. This new arrangement is as much about building the capacity of those who do not participate traditionally in decision-making as about enabling local government officers to engage poor people, inspire, build confidence and trust, and work genuinely in partnership to achieve shared goals.

HOW IT'S ALL LAID OUT

The case studies broadly relate to a number of common neighbourhood renewal themes, such as capacity-building, sustainability, measuring impact, partnerships and initiatives in areas not usually associated with poverty – such as rural communities. Case studies within the book have come from a number of sources, including local government, community organisations, colleges and Councils for Voluntary Service, so that although some are clearly grass-roots developments, others are developed in a local authority framework.

Few issues thrown up through this case study book could be described as unique; in fact, the case studies demonstrate the universal nature of many of the challenges faced by learners, community activists and local government workers.

Practically all community organisations face the challenge of sustaining exciting, effective and innovative projects and services, whether they are in London, Northumberland, Norwich or Bradford. Similarly, measuring the impact of adult and community education, if it is at all measurable, throws up many common issues in Bristol, Leicester, Liverpool and Southampton. The case study book examines a range of projects in all of these geographical areas.

Understanding what neighbourhood renewal itself is about can be a problem. A recent Audit Commission report (June 2002) noted that:

> **...the plethora of initiatives and their complexity makes it difficult to use mainstream services to meet the needs of those living in deprived areas...the neighbourhood renewal message is not getting through to middle managers and front line staff.**

If neighbourhood renewal causes confusion and lack of understanding for local government workers, then people in community groups are likely to be equally confused, particularly because the flow of information is often from local authority to community-based individuals and organisations. This explains why, from the perspective of residents, there is currently conflict, lack of trust and, in some instances, lack of impact in areas that have had significant investment through New Deal for Communities initiatives, for example.

The last selection of case studies contains the voices of people in various communities – people who actively are engaged at the cutting edge. These case studies reflect their frustrations, fears, cynicism and lack of trust in regeneration. They also contain concern, hope and dedication. The case studies are 'active', because they are the experiences and views of people who want to make a difference, but who are frustrated by processes that often seem to take too long and yield little in the short-term.

The case studies are divided into a number of sections, although a number of case studies could be grouped under several different headings. A case study grouped under 'meeting the needs of people who are black or from minority groups' may also be about adult learning, partnerships, and research and working with residents. The following headings are used:

1 Enabling and preparing residents for participation

2 Meeting the needs of people who are black or from minority groups

3 Women: learning the skills for active engagement.

4 Base-line research, providing the right learning opportunities

5 Reaching out into communities

6 Neighbourhood renewal in residential areas

7 Adult and community learning, neighbourhood renewal and the economy

8 Seafaring and neighbourhood renewal

9 Community activists

NEIGHBOURHOOD RENEWAL CASE STUDIES

What is special about this collection of case studies? It is mainly their focus: on the role of adult and community learning in neighbourhood renewal. Without the education of adults, neighbourhood renewal is impossible. This is demonstrated consistently through the case studies, whether learning is taking place on a formal or informal basis. Neighbourhood renewal can't wait for the results of activities to engage the young, raising levels of attainment from Key Stage 1 onwards; adults have to be engaged now!

Without learning, for example, it would have been impossible for a group of local residents in a rural area of Northumberland successfully to have argued and bid for financial support for an extension to the village hall so they could retain their post office. Retaining the post office meant learning about developing constitutions, consulting with local residents, corresponding with various government departments and learning to bid for financial support. The villagers' post office was not only about neighbourhood renewal; it was also about community survival.

To reach a situation where no one is seriously disadvantaged by where they live, in order to 'tackle crime and the causes of crime' and in order to reduce the gap between the poorest in our society and the rest of the population, adults have to learn. This is not reflected in any overt manner within neighbourhood renewal strategies. There are, for example, no public sector agreements for adult learning. Targets only emphasis the importance of raising levels of achievement for children of statutory school age.

There is acknowledgment of the importance of improving basic skills in adults. This is key government strategy. But it is taken for granted that improved environment, reduced worklessness and greater levels of participation in decision-making about the future of communities and the development of better transport infrastructures will take place as a matter of course.

Each case study speaks for itself and is more about the voice of the individual or group of individuals or partners who developed the initiative or project being described than the voice of the learner. However, the success of any initiative can only be measured in terms of its outcomes, which are first and foremost for the benefit of the individual learner, with benefits intended for a neighbourhood or community. Case studies include quotes from learners, details about achievements, destinations and the type of provision offered to adults in various parts of the country.

The success of any of the initiatives included in this book cannot be fully assessed in the short-term, but clearly many thousands of neighbourhood renewal-type initiatives are taking place up and down the country, tens of thousands of adults are learning and there is enough commitment from a whole range of sectors to ensure that neighbourhood renewal is more likely to work this time around.

WORKING IN PARTNERSHIP

A consistent theme running through most of the case studies is that of partnerships. Regeneration initiatives cannot be successful unless they are developed through partnerships. Partnerships cannot be successful unless they are fully representative, and they very rarely are! This often causes disquiet, and a feeling from those who live in ailing neighbourhoods that their involvement is tokenistic – designed primarily to hit on a number of public sector agreements, particularly those around community engagement and consultation.

In such circumstances, the new language of neighbourhood renewal begins to sound hollow and buzzwords and phrases like 'social capital', 'community capacity-building', 'joined-up thinking to joined-up solutions' and 'putting the poorest in our society in the driver's seat' – but for safety putting a lock on the steering wheel and certainly not allowing access to the accelerator pedal – begin to feel patronising. Cynicism sets in.

But people involved in regeneration initiatives are positive, innovative and committed, constantly exploring new possibilities for leavening in funding, seeking accreditation and influencing local and national policies. This is particularly true at neighbourhood level where people, secure in the knowledge that they are best placed to effect positive change in their own life chances and those of their neighbours, constantly strive to make neighbourhood renewal work.

Neighbourhood renewal, as defined by the Government's neighbourhood renewal strategy document (January 2001), is different to previous regeneration initiatives and has considerable potential in developing partnerships and getting them to work effectively. The recognition and genuine desire that the government seems to have for partnership working is the only sensible way of effecting change in Britain's poorest communities.

Coupling partnerships to a long-term strategy adds value. Viewing neighbourhood renewal, and providing financial support for it, over a period of 10 to 20 years recognises that, given the complexity and severity of poverty in our poorest communities, there is no short-term solution to what is a structural and deep-rooted problem. Hence the development of various programmes, plans and initiatives in education, health, employment and crime reduction, and the corresponding public sector agreements that accompany them.

Joining things up, working in partnership, having a long-term strategy and money to support it and of course recognising the importance of the perspectives and involvement of those living in poverty are what make neighbourhood renewal different this time and provide enormous potential for turning things around.

-1-

ENABLING

AND PREPARING

RESIDENTS

FOR

PARTICIPATION

MAGPIE RESOURCE LIBRARY
Getting set for active citizenship

> Through community self-help, everybody wins – the individual, the local community, the providers of formal public services and society as a whole. But it needs careful and patient cultivation: by definition, this is activity done by local communities, not for or to them. Ill-judged, poorly directed or even over-enthusiastic intervention will smother rather than support community involvement. Sensitive, well-judged and supportive assistance will increase community potential and repay the investment many times over.
>
> POLICY ACTION TEAM 19 – COMMUNITY SELF-HELP

THE MAGPIE RESOURCE LIBRARY, situated in the heart of Deptford, is a hive of activity. It comprises a group of committed individuals, all of whom are involved in neighbourhood renewal initiatives of one kind or another. These initiatives involve people in a range of activities – from getting ready for active citizenship through thinking about the development of a community council to thinking about environmental issues by exploring the impact of traffic flow on the local community and investigating innovative ways to 'calm traffic'. All members of Magpie's staff have in common a commitment to Deptford – to making a difference in Deptford – and the knowledge that local people have the potential to make their community a better place to live.

Deptford is a tight-knit community, and Magpie adds to the rich tapestry of cultural diversity, new and old urban renewal and property development initiatives. It achieves this by linking, for example, its active citizenship initiatives with the local market, its lifelong learning strategy with the local nursery and crèche (located in the Albion Arts Centre), and its strategy for engaging young people with various youth outreach programmes.

Magpie is a London-based initiative that operates from rented offices in New Cross Road. Magpie started out in 1996 as a resource library that worked in partnership with Goldsmiths College, the Deptford History Group and the Deptford Community Forum to promote active citizenship. Magpie now is an independent charity that promotes active local citizenship in and around Deptford and New Cross. It is a:

> hub of community information, advice and support, focusing on planning, regeneration. Heritage and environmental protection and assisting with project development and fundraising for identified local needs. (Magpie Annual Report, 2001)

Magpie works to overcome barriers to participation and to support people who traditionally have been excluded from decision-making. It does this very effectively by enthusing people, providing them with the skills to participate, nurturing them and then harnessing their skills. Magpie operates on the principle that the best people to ensure effective regeneration in the community are its residents. Its role is to help people realise how valuable they are and to equip them with tools with which they can demonstrate this.

REGENERATION

Deptford and New Cross have been the focus of more than 20 different regeneration initiatives, involving more than £200 million of public money. Yet local people have not been involved in decision-making.

> **Even more importantly, the lessons of each experience seem to be forgotten and the same mistakes are made again and again. (*Get Set For Citizenship*, 2000)**

Magpie set out to make it possible for local people to find out about the projects and associated problems of the past, what is happening in the present and what might be on the cards for the future. Armed with this knowledge, Magpie believes that people in local communities stand a chance of making neighbourhood renewal what it ought to be – the culmination of decades of experience.

The people who work at Magpie recognise the importance of planning and the need for it to be the most transparent of all processes: often, planning is the most opaque of services, with a bewildering array of unfamiliar terminology and acronyms.

> **You can't see through it and you can't get around it; for community groups on the ground it can feel like swimming in treacle. (Magpie Annual Report, 2001)**

Involvement in decision-making about land use is fundamental to active involvement in planning. Communities can lose vital assets through lack of information and understanding about planning systems.

ANNE HAXELL (GENERAL MANAGER, MAGPIE RESOURCE LIBRARY) AND TERRY HARDY (CREATIVE OUTREACH WORKER)

Magpie is concerned with and interested in heritage and the environment, arguing that heritage has a special significance and importance for poor neighbourhoods, because it provides a source of community pride, inspiration, social cohesion and action. In challenging environmental inequality, Magpie has teamed up with the Deptford Discovery Team, which aims to develop local citizen-led action plans to preserve and refurbish fields and open spaces. These aims contrast directly with permissions granted to allow the loss of open spaces and private sector developments. In this way, in the words of Jess Steele (Magpie's Strategic Director), Magpie promotes 'renewal without destruction, understanding what's already there before you master-plan into oblivion'.

Armed with a clear-cut philosophy of involving people at the community level in decision-making and equipped with detailed research information initiated by Magpie and Deptford Community College (A Decade In Deptford, 1998), Magpie identified the failure of previous regeneration initiatives in Deptford. The next step was to look at ways of encouraging local residents themselves to explore problems and potential solutions within their own communities and then to decide on the most appropriate course of action.

ADULT LEARNING THROUGH THE NX PROJECT

Preparatory work to help local people decide on the future of Deptford involved getting the people to develop new skills. To be effective, this needed the use of new training techniques, and it prompted the development of the Adult and Community Learning Fund (ACLF) and the NX Project. Magpie initially hoped to recruit 16–25 local people to this project, but final numbers far surpassed early hope. In June 1999, volunteers started a 12-week training course to develop skills ranging from research and interview techniques through event planning to participatory rapid appraisal techniques. One year later, these learners were at the heart of the successful Get Set for Citizenship bid for money from the Single Regeneration Budget: local community activists were granted 1.5 million for community work.

THE GET SET PROGRAMME

When Magpie started the NX Project, the expectation was that local residents would describe local problems and barriers to participation and would devise solutions that could be included in a substantial bid for regeneration funding. Local residents did identify problems and solutions, but one message came through louder than all others: 'We do not want any more money until we can be sure that there will be genuine ongoing community control over local regeneration.' As a result, Magpie arranged a short, sharp, preparatory programme to build an infrastructure for the future. Magpie's staff, trainees, associates and partners collaborated to put together the Get Set for Citizenship bid, which focused on skills, structures, social capital, strategies and ongoing creative outreach.

Creative outreach – the Burger Bar

Seeing is believing, and the Magpie Burger Bar must be seen to be believed. This is an example of innovation and creativity that illustrates that there is always a way to get people involved. As Jess Steele noted:

There is a way to reach everyone, it just takes time, imagination and perseverance…their apathy is a poor excuse to hide the failure of your outreach.

Situated in various locations, but often found in the local market, the Burger Bar takes the concept of selling and turns it on its head. It is a fully operational, mobile vehicle that looks like it might be selling burgers, fries and drinks, but wording beautifully painted all over its panels suggests otherwise. The Burger Bar is 'driving democracy' and 'gearing people up for active citizenship'. The outreach workers who operate it are not looking to sell anything – they use the Burger Bar as an opportunity to market ideas, to reach local people and most of all to get people to think about a community council for Deptford, which would be housed in a purpose-built centre.

Magpie describes the Burger Bar as part of its continuous, ambitious and inventive outreach techniques, but it's more than this – it is about valuing people and making sure they know that what they say and how they feel counts. The community council will be made up of mothers, fathers, sisters and brothers, so people are encouraged to think about the qualities of their relatives and to use these as criteria for deciding who they would like to govern local services and resolve community issues.

Magpie supports individuals and small organisations by helping them gear up for regeneration, access funds and devise business plans, etc. This support often involves informal learning processes, leading by example, (gently) pushing and various initiatives such as:

■ pathways: intensive one-to-one support in addressing barriers and making learning opportunities explicit

■ project support: support to help community groups and others turn bright ideas into viable projects

■ neighbourhood development: support to identify 'natural neighbourhoods' and encourage groups of neighbours to define, initiate and manage their own improvement programmes

■ governance: help to create consensus-building structures that are rooted in community realities outside the adversarial realm of party politics.

MORE INNOVATION AND LEARNING

Magpie looks for solutions to universal regeneration problems, such as how to successfully engage local residents in local strategic partnerships without alienating them after their first meeting – a professional meeting may be daunting and can be enough to put people off for life. Magpie likes colour and to challenge routine, and it understands the importance of holding on to people once they have taken the first steps toward becoming involved.

The "problem wall" and "decision tree" are used when residents come to meetings. The residents are encouraged to explore the range of issues currently facing their community and to post them on a wall – the problem wall. Participants arrive at solutions through discussion, and these are then placed on a tree – the decision tree. The whole exercise is very visual and colourful, and participants can take a step back to see the results of their deliberations and reflect on the processes involved. Although not necessarily the mode of operation of the average local strategic partnership, the same decision-making processes are involved. The exercise takes place in a safe and welcoming environment, and people immediately become involved, without feeling left out and alienated.

The learning experiences described prepare and equip residents to get involved. When used alongside techniques such as the Magpie 'Moodometer', which measures participants' feelings before and after meetings (and allows residents to reflect on why they feel as they do), they provide a powerful tool for engagement.

Ultimately, Magpie aims to end the cycle of regeneration failure, while ensuring that regeneration and neighbourhood management programmes are based firmly on local people's priorities. Once structures, skills and social capital are accumulated, local people can manage local regeneration. Magpie recognises that:

> **regeneration and community development are genuine learning experiences. With the right training and support, local residents can gain high quality transferable skills while serving their own communities, improving their own neighbourhoods and establishing a local workforce.** (*Get Set For Citizenship,* 2000)

This workforce will be essential for successful neighbourhood renewal, which needs community-based skills. Local people in Deptford are the researchers for, and will be the planners and managers of, their own regeneration programme.

Magpie is not unique in its problems, which are universal and replicated in all communities that have had neighbourhood renewal initiatives enforced on them. Magpie is unique in how it tackles these problems, and it provides a model of good practice and lessons that can be applied nationally.

Wansbeck Council for Voluntary Services
Customised training services
for community organisations

"The consensus of home research is that something in the region of three to six active community groups per thousand population represents a reasonably healthy level of community activity. Guidance from the Community Development Fund has suggested that from a starting point of five percent in community activity by local people, a reasonable five-year target might be 15 per cent involvement."

POLICY ACTION TEAM 9 – COMMUNITY SELF-HELP

STRATEGIC DEVELOPMENTS IN WANSBECK

WANSBECK COUNCIL FOR VOLUNTARY SERVICE (CVS) covers the Wansbeck district and surrounding area – a relatively small geographical district. Traditionally, most people worked in mining and its associated industries, because the area encompassed several collieries. However, the area has been affected by the gradual closure of collieries between the 1960s and the final closure in Ashington in the 1990s. Although one deep mining colliery remains at Ellington, it employs fewer people than before, because it too is going into decline. The closure of the coalmines in the last 20 years has resulted in the loss of 8,500 jobs. Ashington is twenty-seventh in the national list of most-deprived local authorities, and the unemployment rate for the area as a whole is 9.2 per cent.

About 62,000 people live in Wansbeck. All of the wards in the district are in the top quarter of the most deprived wards in the country, with a significant number in the top 10 per cent. Local Education Action Zones, Health Action Zones (HAZ) and Sure Start Initiatives have been set up in the area. Wansbeck receives funding for neighbourhood renewal, so a local strategic partnership had to be set up and fully operational as a matter of priority. The area's Community Empowerment Fund is managed by the CVS through the Voluntary and Community Sector Network. The Neighbourhood Renewal Fund is supported and managed by the District Council and Northumberland County Council.

The local strategic partnership, which has been accredited by Government Office North East, comprises six local community partnerships, each of which will be represented on the board of the Local Strategic Partnership once it is fully established. Six themed groups serve the board, each addressing one of the key issues of crime and disorder, community, youth, learning, quality of life, the environment and economic renewal. Every community partnership will be represented in the themed groups as well as on the board, as will the Voluntary and Community Sector Network.

WANSBECK CVS

I spoke to Sheila McGuckin, Chief Executive Officer, and Viv Schwartzberg, Project Development Worker, to find out more about the work of Wansbeck CVS. I particularly wanted to find out how the CVS supported local community groups and contributed to the neighbourhood renewal agenda. Sheila had been in her post for six years, and she explained that voluntary sector organisations were relatively underdeveloped in the early days of her employment. The National Lottery was emerging at the time, and community groups were concerned about getting access to funding.

Sheila applied for support so that she could employ a funding officer to help community groups with their funding applications. It transpired, however, that many groups were not in a position to apply for funding, because they did not have appropriate structures in place. This meant that some preparatory work was needed.

The CVS submitted an application for funding to the European Social Fund (ESF). This funding was to enable the CVS to work with community groups to build infrastructures and prepare them to form organisations, become legal entities and bid for support to run services needed in their communities. Sheila informed me that:

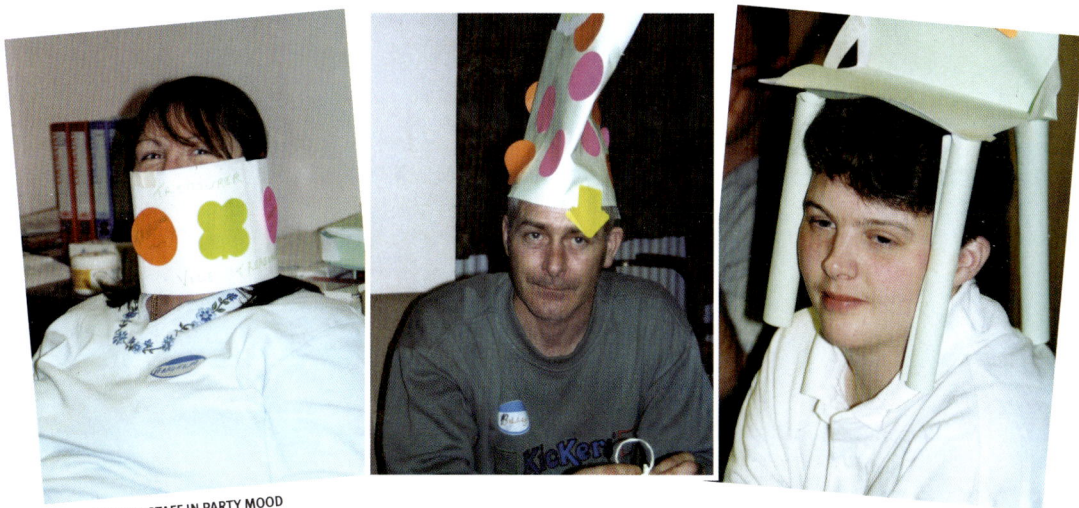

WANSBECK CVS STAFF IN PARTY MOOD

We provided long and short courses, some accredited through the Open College Federation, on how to be a better trustee, managing a community group, etc. We also ran one-day courses on fundraising and bookkeeping. All of this was governed by hard outputs, and this caused problems. The funding limited the number of people who could participate and we could not include people over 65. The funding was also rigid in that it did not allow the possibility of customising courses. This was a major drawback, as we recognised that there were groups of people at different stages of development and knowledge, hence the need for tailor-made training services.

In partnership with community development staff from the local authority and HAZ, the CVS carried out a survey and facilitated meetings to find out what kind of training people in the local area wanted. Some difficulties were encountered in gaining access to community groups to talk to them about training, and time allowed only limited action research. However, the responses obtained were sufficient to work up a provisional training programme focusing on short training courses or one-day events for delegates from different community groups.

Adult and Community Learning Fund

The Community Group Training Project was supported by the fifth round of funding from the Adult and Community Learning Fund (ACLF) which ended in March 2002. When Viv Schwartzberg joined as a training officer, the project had only nine months remaining.

Viv recognised that the way training was sold to people was very significant, so community organisations were sent a letter that did not mention training but offered groups help to take stock of their progress, deal with issues or problems and carry out important tasks. As a result of this letter, people came to the CVS to ask for advice and support or to request a visit from Viv, who would meet them at a time and place that suited them – often evenings or weekends in people's homes.

These meetings led to customised training that was negotiated and delivered for each specific group. Word of mouth was a most effective means of communication after the first letters were sent out, as individuals and people from community groups became aware of the services that Wansbeck CVS offered. Training workshops were organised for people from across Wansbeck, but in a manner essentially different to the model used during the first three months of the ACLF project, when uptake had been disappointing.

Viv recalls the first meeting to discuss how training opportunities should be provided after she arrived:

> **It made sense to provide generic sessions alongside customised training for individual organisations, but it was agreed that these would be more successful if they were less frequent, networking events rather than skills-based courses. Each event would focus on a common issue identified from the customised training with individual groups. When we did our first networking event, we had a very big turn out, which showed we had made the right decision. As expected, the areas in which people wanted customised training were wide ranging: group or project development review, training needs identification, policy development, firming up management committee skills, conflict resolution, running an AGM [Annual General Meeting] – everything. You name it, there was a group that wanted it – and they each needed it at different times and for different purposes. That is what generally makes area-wide, capacity building, training courses impractical for community activists.**

The nature of community organisations in Wansbeck

Recognising how community organisations tend to develop, Sheila explained that the CVS decided to provide a range of services into which people could dip in and out as and when necessary – and depending on the organisation's stage of development. Clear and identifiable processes and milestones are involved in the development of a community organisation: from clarifying an idea and turning it into a plan through writing a constitution and setting up policies, systems and structures to applying for funding once the organisation has established its remit and client group. The next stage is the tricky issue of sustaining the organisation, and the final stage is to provide support facilities for staff, so that they are best able to service the needs of the identified client group and are knowledgeable about new (government and local) initiatives.

Viv also highlighted the importance of coordinating the support provided to community groups. At any one time, Wansbeck CVS offers a variety of services to community organisations. Within the CVS, the work is very much team-oriented, with officers specialising in, among other things, project development and management, funding information, community development and outreach, marketing and promotion, and widening participation.

COMMUNITY MEDIATION SERVICE

The Community Mediation Service illustrates the coordinated way in which the CVS works to build the capacity of individuals and groups and to enable them to have a greater impact in a wide range of areas, including decision-making and neighbourhood renewal. In an experiment set up by the Crime and Disorder Partnership, six people were trained as volunteer mediators with the help of a one-off grant. The volunteers decided to keep the project going when the funding ran out, so they came to the CVS to find out what was involved. They took part in some customised training activities that gave them insight into the demands of setting up and running a community organisation and that helped to identify their training needs.

Members of the Community Mediation Service realised that they had to start at the beginning, by piecing together a constitution that enshrined the purpose, principles and long-term vision for their work. They then needed to work out a development plan, a funding and promotion strategy and an action plan – all based on evidence of need and the appropriate means for meeting it – that could be combined into a three- to five-year business plan. They operated according to Viv's 'clearly identifiable processes'. Viv explains:

They're at the stage now of writing their different funding applications, based on sound planning and an understanding of the management implications. So far they have completed three applications that have gone in to various trusts. At the moment, I am supporting them as they prepare the applications, but in a few months' time they will be writing them by themselves and just using me to proofread them or advise about particular issues – the way they do with Stephen, our Funding Information Officer.

The process the Community Mediation Service members took part in helped them gain recognition for past work and expertise. The chairperson is very active in the Crime and Disorder Reduction Partnership, and he has been elected to represent his local community partnership in one of the themed groups of the local strategic partnership.

The research into social policy issues and developments that the group was encouraged to carry out to support bids for funding did not just excite them and make them more determined to pursue their goals. It meant that the chairperson is able to speak with more authority and to have a greater impact in meetings. Viv notes:

Research and planning, knowing the field, is essential; people are much more creative when they properly examine the details of the initiative they are thinking about and can see it in the wider context. There is no substitute for going through this learning and development process.

Community Link Project

The CVS also has a Community Link Project that aims to engage people in voluntary work, to prepare them to contribute towards particular voluntary and community organisations and to encourage them to get involved with their local community partnerships. The CVS provides volunteers with intensive support that draws heavily on the experience of the ACLF project. Some volunteers decide to join community groups and to go through the clearly identifiable processes that lead to the development of community organisations or to represent such organisations in decision-making bodies.

Measuring impact

The real measure of the effectiveness of Wansbeck CVS relates to a wide range of outputs and outcomes including:

- the extent to which the CVS realises its main aim – the development of sustainable and well-run organisations

- the number of people who have helped to develop management committees, devised constitutions, policies and plans, and applied successfully for funding by taking advantage of training opportunities

- the number of organisations that have used the service, how often and the number and range of courses taken up

- the number of people who have made a commitment to the accredited learning programme that the CVS uses as the framework for all its customised and generic capacity-building training

- the number of people engaged in networks and public decision-making as a result of their learning experience.

It is clear that measurement of the impact and effectiveness of an organisation or service and its ability to effect change, for example through training opportunities, is a formative process. At certain points during the development of a group, it is possible to assess competence through the way people deal with real tasks, situations and problems that demand specific knowledge and skills. You can observe the contribution individuals make to group decisions and how the group works as a unit. You can examine how effective the management committee is in carrying out its duties, whether the group has drawn up the relevant policies and knows how to implement them, if the group can evaluate its work and how well the group meets the needs of its client groups.

Wansbeck has about 200 groups, and the CVS has worked with most of them. Some just require information on new initiatives – the Community Empowerment Fund, for example – and such information is sent out through a regular newsletter; others access help as and when it is needed. Support may be intensive or may simply involve finding the relevant document – like a framework or set of guidelines – in a file. Importantly, everything is offered free of charge, which helps to make services inclusive.

Bite Size courses

The CVS offered a wide range of courses as part of the Learning and Skills Council-funded Bite Size initiative in 2002. The CVS used this opportunity creatively, and Viv ran a number of courses on how to get important things done for community organisations. A core group of six people who came to all of the events did not want the sessions to end, and they decided to set up the Project Support Group, which now meets once a month. This illustrates how a taste of education can lead to greater levels of interest and can provide a catalyst for self-help and community organisation.

Community Action, Development and Management

All of the capacity-building training offered through the CVS is locked into the framework of an accredited programme called Community Action, Development and Management. This programme has National Vocational Qualification (NVQ) Level 3 equivalence, but it is designed to be flexible and is customised for community settings. The modules or elements do not have to be completed in any set order, and the assessment process is user-friendly. Aspects of becoming an effective management committee can be mixed, matched and delivered in a way that suits the organisation and the actual tasks they have to complete. The outcomes of all training sessions are recorded and stored, and every participant can use the products of group activities as evidence of learning.

The CVS organised and ran a three-day residential course in March 2002. During this course, the core elements of capacity-building were explored, so that groups could assess their own achievement and skills and could identify further training needs with the criteria described in the accredited framework. The event attracted large numbers of participants and supported the development of a range of community initiatives such as the 'Our PART Project'.

Participative action research

Through the Community Empowerment Fund, Wansbeck CVS decided to set up a participative action research team, known as the Our PART Project. The main aim of this project was to train volunteers recruited from local community groups to research how local people want to be involved in making decisions that affect their lives and what resources and services they need and want in their areas. Initially, two teams were trained to carry out separate pieces of research – a group of local parents and a group of young, travelling people. The groups learned the methods and skills of participative action research: how to design research questions, to decide on a sample, to conduct structured interviews and to analyse and report the results. Furthermore, the training provided fell within one of the modules of the Community Action, Development and Management's accredited programme, which enabled participants to work towards the nationally recognised certificate.

The work of the first two teams paved the way for the Our PART Project, and over 40 people have come forward to be trained as researchers. These include the original teams and people they interviewed or who had heard about the success of their work.

The CVS uses a model based on research methods developed in the UK and in the US to give people on whom research is focused a leading role in its design and delivery. The concept behind participative action research is that most community-based research, although ethically sound, is grounded in a culture far removed from the experience of the people who are its focus and that they have little control over how the research is constructed or conducted. This concept is clearly what neighbourhood renewal is all about, particularly because work carried out through the CVS acknowledges that there is no substitute for getting local people to work out their own solutions for tackling local problems and issues.

The major focus for Wansbeck's participative action research team now is to find out the local people's opinions and ideas about the key issues for neighbourhood renewal for the six community partnerships. As well as investigating what people think about the issues, the research will look into how people from different neighbourhoods feel about being involved in public decision-making. The aim is to empower community representatives in the local strategic partnership, so that they can have more impact on decisions and can influence the way decisions are made. The research-based proposals will not just identify the issues to be addressed but will also recommend actions. Furthermore, the researchers will interview service providers and will run workshops that bring services providers together with local people to look for ways of putting proposals into action.

Sheila informed me that:

Where we have service providers already locked in to partnerships and locally accountable forums, there is a direct route in terms of asking questions about services, planned delivery, etc. The themed groups that service the local strategic partnership all have to come up with action plans – our action research will be informing these plans.

Viv noted just prior to the end of the interview that:

The training starts in earnest this weekend. Project members will serve a long 'apprenticeship'. Skills need to be practiced and honed. By the end of 12 months, they will be seasoned action researchers. All of these people are unemployed or low waged. The plan is to develop the project into a community research and training unit in Wansbeck, run by local people. It means they will be in the driving seat, aware of research methodology, better informed and better able to make decisions. Why have so many external consultants parachuting in and earning huge fees, when some of that money could go back into the local economy? After all, the best potential community researchers already live in Wansbeck.

Liverpool City Council
Equality of opportunity and Community Matters

> Most people associate learning with formal education, in schools, universities or on training course. But neighbourhood renewal is a new challenge, and everyone involved will need to develop new skills. For some, this may involve individual training. But it also means learning from experience, learning jointly with other partners, and talking to people facing similar challenges.
>
> NEIGHBOURHOOD RENEWAL SKILLS AND KNOWLEDGE PROGRAMME, HELPING PEOPLE IMPROVE NEIGHBOURHOODS, DECEMBER 2001

LIVERPOOL IS A WORLD-RENOWNED CITY that is immediately recognisable – from the Liver Birds that adorn the Liver Buildings at the Pier Head to the two cathedrals that dominate its skyline. Liverpool is at the end of the M62 motorway, the end of the railway is at the main-line station Lime Street and the city itself is at the end of the beginning of a major economic regeneration programme – so publicity information would have us believe. Liverpool, according to its Annual Performance Plan 2002/2003, is becoming a world-class city, with proposals for:

> ...a £300 million world-class stadium at Kings dock; a revolutionary £800 million retail development in the Paradise Street development area; a £10 million cruise liner terminal and plans for an iconic building which will stand as a forth grace on the waterfront. The city centre's retail growth rate is one of the fastest in the country and premium rental growth is twice the national average.

Cranes dominate Liverpool's skyline, and the sounds, smells and sights of construction are everywhere, with modern halls of residence being built for its estimated 40,000 students and hotels being erected at a rate of knots. Liverpool's city centre has been the focus of investment and building by at least half a dozen major hotel chains within the last five years. In fact, the city centre has undergone a massive transformation already – even before the 'revolutionary £800 million retail development'.

POVERTY IN THE CITY

Liverpool is also one of the most impoverished and researched places in Western Europe and has had Objective 1 Status since 1994. An estimated 330,000 people in Liverpool (more than

80 per cent of the population) qualify for funding for neighbourhood renewal in accordance with the Government's six indices for deprivation measure, and 28 wards in Liverpool are in the nation's top 10 per cent of most deprived wards. A look around some of Liverpool's inner city areas – for example, Kensington, Dingle, Toxteth and Everton – confirms the city's poverty.

Liverpool is by no means a passive city though, and it has a history of action and community-based organisations. Growing active communities are not needed here, for fully-fledged political activists and thousands of residents are prepared to say exactly what they think about local education authority plans and the City Council's initiatives.

COMMUNITY MATTERS

I met with Colin Watts – Millennium Awards Coordinator and one of the main movers behind the City Council's Community Training Unit over the last ten years. I was particularly interested to find out what training provision the City Council had made available to community organisations so they were better able to function and participate in local democracy. I also wanted to know how equality of opportunity – through the provision of 'value added' support services – contributed towards ensuring a good level of take up for non-traditional trainees.

The Community Matters training programme was set up by officers of Liverpool City Council's Community Development and Equality Unit towards the end of 1990. In January 1991, Colin Watts was appointed to the part-time post of Community Matters Training Coordinator to organise the programme

The main aim of the programme was to assist in the organisational development of community, black and voluntary organisations in Liverpool, by providing a regular programme of short training courses. The programme was funded entirely by the City Council to the tune of about £45,000 a year; this included salaries for the part-time coordinator, training manager and administrative support staff. From the start, all courses were offered free of charge to participants, with support services and additional expenses paid for those who needed them.

In 1995, the programme was extended to provide for the specific needs of organisations and individuals involved in local partnerships in the city. Some funding for this came from the partnerships themselves. In 1995, the Community Matters Training Unit also was established within the Council's Community Development and Equality Unit.

In the same year, the training unit worked with the Federation of Community Work Training Groups, Merseyside Training and Enterprise Council (TEC) and the Liverpool Community College to set up an assessment centre for the newly established NVQ in community work. It was hoped to provide prospective candidates with the necessary underpinning knowledge through a course in basic community work skills that was accredited through the Merseyside Open College Network (MOCN) and was run by the training unit.

Beneficiaries

The target group for all Community Matters training included committee members, activists, staff and volunteers of community, black, resident and voluntary groups in Liverpool. Priority was given to:

- organisations grant-aided by the city council
- non-funded community and residents groups
- smaller voluntary organisations without training budgets.

The training unit maintained a database and mailing list of over 1,000 community and voluntary organisations in the city. Training calendars, application forms, and so on, for each programme were sent out to all organisations.

Every effort was made to ensure that all those who needed to attend were able to do so. It was made clear that participants' organisations were expected to take responsibility for sending participants on courses and to ensure they put what they had learnt to use. If applicants failed to attend without good reason, the organisation was charged the cost of providing their place.

Equality of opportunity

On occasion, Community Matters worked to provide area-based training in a centre acceptable to the organisations taking advantage of the training. More usually, however, training

MANAGING STAFF AND VOLUNTEERS

would be based in the city centre. This was largely in recognition of the 'territorial' nature of many communities and the fact that community activists from the north of the city, for example, were

COLIN WATTS (COMMUNITY MATTERS TRAINING COORDINATOR)

unlikely to attend a training course in the south of the city. The city centre is well served with a good public transport system, most people are familiar with it and those who took advantage of several training sessions got to know the training venues well.

The Community Training Unit worked with a range of trainers: some were part of the Community Matters team, while others – from a core group of trainers – were called on to provide specific training sessions. A panel assessed the suitability of trainers to participate in Community Matters. All trainers were expected to have a good knowledge of Liverpool, its various communities and the issues facing the communities, as well as a good understanding of the needs of those who work in the voluntary and community sectors.

To ensure that potential trainees did not miss out on training opportunities, the training unit established an innovative and effective equal opportunities code of conduct, that was in line with Liverpool City Council's equal opportunities statement. Accordingly, all course were:

- offered free of charge

- run in an informal and relaxed way and in comfortable surroundings

- offered with travel expenses paid for unwaged participants who could not be supported by their organisations

- provided with childcare costs paid for on behalf of participants with children of pre-school age

- run, whenever possible, during school hours and school terms

- run from centres that provided facilities for the deaf

- conducted in plain spoken and written English.

In addition to this, locally based courses were run for those who spoke no English or had English as an additional language. Written work was kept to a minimum on all courses, and all applications for training were monitored to check that the training unit attracted participants who adequately represented the various groups and communities within the city.

Course content

The emphasis of all Community Matters courses was on the effective functioning of the organisations involved rather than on the service they provided or the issues around which they were campaigning. Examples of courses provided were 'Running meetings', 'Financial management', 'Planning and monitoring', 'Recruitment and selection' and 'Managing staff and volunteers'.

The course on basic community work skills, which was accredited through MOCN, lasted 14 days. All other Community Matters courses varied between two-hour briefing sessions to one- to three-day courses, except for 'Planning and Monitoring', which lasted six days and was accredited.

Monitoring and evaluation

The effectiveness of training provision was monitored in a number of ways:

- Participants were invited to give their views on the usefulness of the material, the effectiveness of the teaching and the suitability of the venue, and so on, in users' forums held at the end of each programme.

- Confidential information on sex, race and colour, and employment status, and so on, was collected, analysed and monitored for all programmes.

- Targets set for provided training hours were regularly monitored.

- Regular monitoring and planning meetings were held with officers in the Community Development and Equality Unit who were in regular contact with community and voluntary groups and monitored their performance.

Neighbourhood renewal

The main aim of the Community Training Unit was to improve the capacity of neighbourhood organisations, particularly their ability to provide services effectively and to better represent the interests of their members. The three main strands of its work over the last ten years – Community Matters training programmes, training for local partnerships and training in community work – all are consistent with this aim. This supports the city council's view that building strong neighbourhoods is key to building a strong city.

Colin Watts notes, however, that training is very much a two-way process from a partnership perspective. People in community groups will always need support, and city, county and borough councils are well placed to provide training services because they are informed about government thinking and about local and national policy and strategic developments. Local government, however, comprises individuals with different knowledge, perspectives and experiences. Colin informed me that:

Liverpool
City
Council

> **If you are serious about community development and neighbourhood renewal, then you can't assume that officers have the basic skills and experience to be able to work within the culture of the community that they are going into. These skills have to be acquired; it's very much a two-way process in working with communities and to get organisations to work more effectively and to be able to achieve whatever it is that they want to achieve.**

Future developments

In 2001, the City Council decided to wind down the Community Training Unit, which ceased to function in March 2002. However, the Adult and Lifelong Learning Service of the Council's Education Directorate agreed to take on the work of the Unit. A programme planned for autumn 2002 will closely resemble the model established by the Training Unit.

This change is seen very much as a logical progression, because the Education Directorate plans a multi-pronged, adult learning service for the city. This will include employing neighbourhood outreach workers (for the six 'clustered' partnership districts of the city); their prime tasks will be to develop new learning communities in these districts, to work with local community organisations and pathways partnerships and to develop a district profile, a participation profile and a current delivery map to inform future planning and service delivery.

-2-

MEETING

THE NEEDS

OF PEOPLE

WHO ARE BLACK

OR FROM

MINORITY GROUPS

Community Leadership
Programme

> **70 per cent of all people from ethnic minorities live in the 88 most deprived local authority districts, compared with 40 per cent of the general population.**
>
> A COMMITMENT TO NEIGHBOURHOOD RENEWAL, 2001

> **There is widespread agreement that neighbourhood renewal cannot be successful without the active involvement of the community. Yet community leaders and their organisations do not always receive sufficient funding, support and training to play an effective role. If this were forthcoming, the prospects for the success of neighbourhood renewal would be much greater.**
>
> POLICY ACTION TEAM 16 – LEARNING LESSONS

FUNDED BY THE DEPARTMENT FOR EDUCATION AND SKILLS (DfES), the Bernie Grant Trust runs the Community Leadership Programme. The programme is unique in a number of ways and is the perfect example of an initiative that takes a bottom-up approach by encouraging members of black communities to decide who to put forward for the Community Leadership Programme.

Through this programme, the Bernie Grant Trust recognises that local people know what is most likely to work – as does the government through its Neighbourhood Renewal Strategy. Local people know the local issues, the individuals within their community and the person or people most likely to make a difference in trying to turn around and change the direction of ailing neighbourhoods. In addition, local people have talents and experience as clients and as organisers of services. To fail to tap into this source would be a missed opportunity.

The Community Leadership Programme is part of a national pilot programme. It is an 'organic and flexible capacity building programme for individuals with leadership potential who have been referred to the Trust by other community members' (Stafford Scott, Programme Director). The programme currently runs in two areas of the country with significantly large black communities – Tottenham in London and Moss Side in Manchester.

The broad objectives of the programme are to focus attention on the role of leadership in community regeneration, to build social capital in inner-city communities and to produce a model of best practice that can be replicated in various parts of the country. For the nominated individuals, the programme aims to build their capacity by providing information and opportunities to develop skills within the community. The programme also aims to enable and empower communities to represent themselves effectively, to resolve conflict and to create accountable, effective and responsive leadership.

UNIQUE AND INNOVATIVE

The programme is unique in that it targets those who are most likely to be disenfranchised, who are most likely to live in poverty and who are least likely to be employed and involved in decision-making – people who are black and from minority groups. The Neighbourhood Renewal Strategy estimates that 70 per cent of all people who are black or from minority groups live in the country's 88 most deprived wards. Specifically the programme:

- targets people who are black and from minority group communities

- uses black consultants to work with target groups

- links up with current regeneration initiatives

- links communities in different regeneration areas

- allows participants to shape the programme

- highlights the role of, and develops strategies to challenge, institutional racism

- adopts new recruitment methods.

COMMUNITY LEADERSHIP

The programme developed as a result of a series of discussions within the Bernie Grant Trust about the best way to continue Bernie Grant's legacy by making an effective and worthwhile impact on the black community and its ability to master its own destiny. In particular, the Trust was concerned – as Bernie himself had been – about the source for the next generation of community leaders.

Great concern existed about the way in which funding had been withdrawn from community groups and how this would

LORNA HARSFORD AND DIJONN TAYLOR AT A COMMUNITY LEADERSHIP CONFERENCE

impact on future developments in terms of meeting the needs of local people and enabling organisations to provide services to challenge racism, promote cultural diversity and service the needs of black people. Such developments were especially important given the Government's policy towards greater levels of community engagement, involvement and consultation, particularly with reference to neighbourhood renewal.

With the decimation of communities and the absence of community leadership, the danger of disenfranchised communities being left behind was recognised by the Bernie Grant Trust. Funding was identified for a pilot project in 2000, and work to get the project started began in May 2001.

STAFFORD SCOTT AND TONY GORDON

THE LEADERSHIP COURSE

The leadership course focuses on the importance of black leadership for the future, on community leadership and on the government policy that makes it imperative for black people to be organised to meet the challenges presented by initiatives such as neighbourhood renewal. It consists of five modules. An introduction and the leadership and diversity aspects of the programme are delivered through residential sessions. A discussion group and a workshop explore the way forward for the black community, the development of a strategy to increase participation and how to become more influential with regard to decision-making about the future of communities and the country as a whole.

Alongside these core modules, a series of workshops cover a range of areas, from developing presentation skills and exploring community development issues to fund-raising and financial management – all essential knowledge and information for future community leaders. Participation in the programme usually requires a commitment of at least two days a month for a period of six months.

The managers and tutors of the leadership programme hope that participants who have completed the programme will get actively involved in community issues, particularly those relating to urban regeneration initiatives. In fact, evidence shows that this is happening already as participants gain confidence and understanding from participating in this programme.

DESTINATIONS FOR PARTICIPANTS

Machel Bogues, the Bernie Grant Trust's Development Officer, explained that the project:

…does wonders for the confidence of people, the residential in particular enables our future leaders to come together in a safe and supportive environment to grapple with a range of real-life issues that have a direct bearing on how people live in the black

community. It's also an opportunity for solidarity and for people to realise that they are very valuable with many skills and talents, all of which are necessary qualities in a good leader. From our first programme in Manchester, one of our participants has gone on to work for a youth education programme. When asked if he thought that the programme had given him the tools to do the job, he explained that it had done more than this, as it had enabled him to apply for the job in the first place. In Tottenham, one of our participants was elected secretary of her local residents' association; she explained to me that it was the programme that encouraged her to get involved in local issues.

So far 34 people have joined the leadership programme; 26 of these have completed the programme. Some participants already are engaging in local assemblies in Tottenham and community networks in Moss Side and are working with the police to tackle crime and the causes of crime, by dealing with rising gun violence in Tottenham and black-on-black crime.

Participants also are getting involved in decision-making by meeting heads of service within

A LIVELY AUDIENCE AT THE COMMUNITY LEADERSHIP CONFERENCE, OCTOBER 2002

various City and Borough Council departments and local strategic partnerships. In so doing, they are helping stakeholders develop an awareness and understanding of community issues from a black and grass roots perspective. This is an invaluable insight, because stakeholders can live parallel lives without fully appreciating the issues for black communities.

CHALLENGES AND THE FUTURE

The Trust sees such a programme as an essential way forward for black community members, given that some local authorities are reluctant to engage with people who are black or from minority groups. In the words of Stafford Scott:

There are two issues here: one is a lack of knowledge and the other is a lack of trust – a lack of knowledge on the part of many individuals within the black community and a lack of trust in us from the powers that be.

The Trust acknowledges that many people in black communities are totally unaware of neighbourhood renewal, while those who are demonstrate a healthy scepticism towards it, having had a plethora of regeneration initiatives 'done to them' before. For this reason, learning about the Neighbourhood Renewal Strategy and Community Empowerment Fund is part of the programme of study for participants on the Community Leadership Programme.

The Bernie Grant Trust is realistic about the challenges that it faces through its new programme. It is concerned about how money for neighbourhood renewal is spent, noting, for example, that money for 'the community' from the Community Empowerment Fund is used to employ consultants or goes to established umbrella organisations that are not necessarily representative of and have few, if any, links with black communities. It is hoped that support for the Trust's new programme will break the tendency for funds to go to mainstream education providers that provide community leadership programmes. Stafford Scott is concerned that such institutions are less likely than they think to have dynamic connections within the community and to attract core individuals who can make a difference in tackling poverty, crime, under-achievement and lack of participation.

The Community Leadership Programme proves what the Bernie Grant Trust has always known – that a pool of talent within black and minority group communities in inner cities must be engaged to ensure the success of current regeneration initiatives. The programme confirms this fact for participants and exposes it to stakeholders. Stafford implores that communities 'are crying out for an opportunity to develop their potential and ability to be part of the solution and not just seen as the problem'.

The Bernie Grant Trust has learned through its programme that communities themselves can identify their future leaders and understand the importance of 'engaging' with mainstream service providers. However, the Trust acknowledges that communities cannot be expected to rise to the new challenges of neighbourhood renewal without appropriate support. Such support must be provided by people with the right knowledge, perspective and experience of issues of race and racism.

The need for initiatives such as the Community Leadership Programme cannot be overstated. Such initiatives can work in partnership with mainstream service providers, can put forward true community representatives and can begin the process of developing partnerships, while enhancing and developing the social capital of the communities in which they work.

The message from the Bernie Grant Trust is that sustainability will only be a reality when key stakeholders are able to meet black people and black communities halfway. 'At the moment, there is too much cynicism and mistrust' (Stafford Scott). An open hand is extended in a genuine attempt to heal old wounds and pool resources and expertise in order to challenge the multiple problems plaguing poor neighbourhoods.

YEMENI DEVELOPMENT FOUNDATION
Invisible
minorities

'Community leaders do not get the support and encouragement they need; that professionals are often not equipped to operate effectively in poor neighbourhoods; and that civil servants lack a full understanding of the communities that they are trying to influence. In addition, there is a lack of entrepreneurship, drive and innovation and no reliable way for local organisations to learn from "what works".'

POLICY ACTION TEAM 16 – LEARNING LESSONS

THE YEMENI DEVELOPMENT FOUNDATION (YDF) is based in the Highgate area of Birmingham, which is part of the political ward of Sparkbrook. The area is near the city centre and includes a large number of people who are black and from minority groups. The YDF is housed in Magnolia House, a premises of Matthew Boulton College. The college is a significant partner to the YDF, providing offices and access to various facilities, such as information and communications technology and training rooms.

The YDF is a relatively new organisation that was launched in the House of Lords in February 2000. Its main aim is to meet the needs and support the development of 'invisible communities' – not only individuals and organisations from the Yemen, but also people who do not fall into any obvious government or local authority category with respect to provision of a monitoring service. This includes people who are Algerian, Albanian, Kurdish, Bosnian and Somali. People from these communities who live in Birmingham and elsewhere in the country are invisible not because of their appearance but because their specific and general needs rarely are met.

Mohammad Almasyabi, the chief executive of YDF, explains:

YDF has come into existence after many years of community development involvement and years of close observations and discussions with various groups within the community.

Setting up a development organisation that acts as an Intermediary Support Organisation for Yemeni and other similar 'invisible' disadvantaged groups has become a vital necessity in order to provide a voice and access to mainstream sections of statutory and voluntary sectors.

This sentiment is echoed by the YDF's chairperson, Abdullah Bawhab. He explained that, since the organisation was established, it has constantly expanded its activities and services to community groups, not only in the UK but also in the Yemen. It delivers projects and services that will 'alleviate poverty, reduce disadvantage and provide opportunities for a better and brighter future for our target groups'.

THE YEMENI COMMUNITY

The history of the Yemeni community in Britain can be traced back to 1885, when it was the first Arab community and one of the first ethnic groups to settle in the UK. At that time, the community comprised mostly single men who worked as sailors and donkey workers in the British Merchant Navy. Yemeni men gradually began working in the steel industry, foundries and factories. Some men married British women, but others preferred to live a 'semi-single life' and to visit their wives and families in the Yemen, as and when they could.

In the 1970s, the Yemeni men lost their jobs as industry went into decline, and many left the UK to make their way to the Gulf States and US in search of better job prospects. The current Yemeni community is estimated to include 30,000–40,000 people, and a national network of organisations is developing. The community still consists predominantly of men working in the steel industry, mainly in Birmingham and Sheffield, although many Yemeni men have set up their own businesses – mainly corner shops and grocery stores. The YDF recognises the need to provide the Yemeni community with support that enables its members to explore a wider range of opportunities and to have more involvement in decision-making and in influencing the direction of their own families and neighbourhoods.

MEETING THE NEEDS OF INVISIBLE COMMUNITIES

In order to meet this need, the YDF established a wide range of courses, surgeries and one-to-one sessions for members of various Yemeni communities and other invisible communities. The YDF currently supports 32 community groups – mainly in and around Birmingham – and a number of organisations based in the Yemen. Various newsletters, including the YDF's monthly funding newsletter, are used to inform community organisations about new courses and about new national and local initiatives likely to effect the establishment and development of organisations.

The monthly newsletter often prompts people to call the YDF for information on funding. For example, someone from a community group looking through the newsletter reads about the new Community Fund Strategic Plan. They decide that they want to know more about the fund and how to apply for financial support, and they contact the YDF for more information.

The YDF is very flexible in how it responds to the needs of its client organisations. It provides generic training for all organisations on how to achieve registered charity status, provides information through dissemination events on new training opportunities, holds surgeries and provides individual needs-based analysis sessions on request. In addition, members from client organisations can simply drop in to the YDF's offices. On one hand, the YDF is led by the needs of its client organisations; on the other, it is aware of global issues and their importance for community development.

The YDF keeps a file containing a range of information for each organisation; this enables services to be individually tailored. Typical details held by the YDF are:

- all correspondence with the organisation

- evidence forms that detail the work and support given to each client group

- information on fundraising activities and grant applications

THE YEMENI DEVELOPMENT FOUNDATION LAUNCH, HOUSE OF LORDS, JULY 2001

- all current and completed project activities

- public relations and promotion activities

- skills and training needs, including assessments of all activities

- quality assurance protocols and systems development

- financial records and budgeting information

- business and strategic plans

- legal structure and constitution documents.

THE ROLE OF ADULT LEARNING

All of the learning that takes place through the YDF is practical in its application. It supports members of invisible communities in areas such as developing constitutions, writing bids, implementing quality assurance procedures, becoming more effective and playing a more-informed role in decision-making processes. These services are delivered by a range of trainers; some are contracted in because they work in a particular specialist training area, some are provided by Matthew Boulton College and the YDF also provides its own training.

The YDF measures its impact through the intimate relations it has with its client groups and by monitoring and evaluating the training it delivers. This information is supported by feedback from the one-to-one, needs-led sessions and from members of client organisations that drop in to the offices. The YDF is not satisfied with this, though; it wants to measure 'third-party impact', which requires feedback from the people supported by its client organisations.

This is another demonstration of the YDF's ever-changing and responsive approach to meeting the needs of its client groups as well as the demands of funders, who require increasingly more information on the impact of services. To help it assess 'third-party impact', the YDF is bidding for funding so it can offer an outreach service – yet another important prong in the multi-pronged strategy to provide quality services and measure impact. Outreach workers will gain valuable insight into the experiences and needs of the people supported by the YDF's client organisations and will offer additional support.

ACHIEVEMENTS AND FUTURE DEVELOPMENTS

The YDF has achieved a great deal in the last two and a half years, but it is not a service that rests on its laurels. Since the YDF was established, a range of grassroots organisations has asked the YDF to provide support for a range of training and development services. The YDF has facilitated the establishment of six voluntary organisations that assist and support their communities and has provided a series of governance and management training sessions for volunteers, staff and management committee members of several organisations.

In terms of future developments, the YDF is thinking locally and acting globally. The Yemeni government has asked the YDF to deliver services to target groups in the Yemen, for example to provide training in capacity building and in skill development for children in the labour market and poverty-affected men.

The YDF also is mindful of the problems and needs of its invisible communities in Britain – their poverty and the support needed to alleviate poverty and encourage self-help and participation. The YDF plays a central role in effecting change locally by providing training opportunities, facilitating access (for example, to resources) and generally offering a listening ear and a flexible and responsive approach to meeting local needs.

Yemeni
Development
Foundation

KEIGHLEY HEALTHY LIVING NETWORK
Feeling good about learning

'The Government is committed to ensuring that communities' needs and priorities are at the fore in neighbourhood renewal and that residents of poor neighbourhoods have the tools to get involved in whatever way they want.'

A NEW COMMITMENT TO NEIGHBOURHOOD RENEWAL –

NATIONAL STRATEGY ACTION PLAN, 2001

KEIGHLEY

KEIGHLEY, WEST YORKSHIRE, is a former industrial mill town with a distinctly traditional atmosphere. It is a large town with all the usual services and facilities associated with modern towns – a purpose-built covered shopping centre, high-rise car parks and a large college – but it also has a rural feel. Just two minutes drive from the town centre is a very rural area with traditional stone cottages, narrow minor roads and open countryside. However, Keighley does suffer from many of the problems associated with inner city areas, despite its rural setting.

Keighley is also a place of contrasts in terms of the people that live there. Located about ten miles from Bradford, it has significant Pakistani and Bangladeshi communities. The summer of 2001 in Keighley saw none of the disturbances that were seen in Bradford and Oldham, but the town does consist of 'parallel communities' that have few points of reference and even fewer points of contact. Overall, 22 per cent of people in the area are from various minority groups; although a few families are Chinese, African-Caribbean and Indian, the biggest minority groups comprise Pakistani families followed by Bangladeshi families.

Around 68,000 people live in Keighley and its immediate district. Two-thirds of the area is rural, and it has two wards in the top 10 per cent of most deprived districts in the country – South Keighley and West Keighley. These wards also have Objective 2 Status; this has caused some friction between poor white communities and Asian communities, because South and West Keighley include mainly Asian families. Round 6 of the Single Regeneration Budget (SRB) is active in Keighley, but this is new to the area, which has not benefited from previous rounds of SRB funding.

In the 1950s and 1960s, a number of people from Pakistan came to Keighley to work in the foundries and mills. Bangladeshi people came to work in the 1960s, and their families followed in the 1970s. Unemployment rates in the area generally are not particularly high, although local industries – most of which are small- to medium-sized engineering firms – do not pay well and provide insecure employment. A dynamic relationship still exists between Keighley and Pakistan, with people regularly travelling between the two places. Keighley is thought of as a model community in Pakistan, and a significant number of men come there to marry and work.

Real fear also exists in Keighley. Four murders have been committed recently – all four were almost certainly related to drugs. In Keighley you can buy some of the cheapest heroin in the country; the drug dealers are mainly Asian and the drug users are all white. Tensions between the communities heightened after the terrorist attack on the World Trade Centre in New York on 11 September 2001: wearing a Hijab can be a dangerous practice in the wrong part of Keighley.

KEIGHLEY HEALTHY LIVING CENTRE

For a town of its size, Keighley has a disproportionately large number of voluntary sector groups (nearly 300). Although this does demonstrate a culture of self-help, it is not necessarily a good thing, because the smallest of cultural groups has its own centre and local communities have tended to develop in a compartmentalised fashion. This has had implications for the Keighley Healthy Living Network (KHLN) and how it provides its services.

I met with Jill Kibble, manager of the Keighley Healthy Living Centre, and Hawarun Hussain, project worker, to find out more about Keighley. I particularly wanted to learn about the work carried out in the Centre and the variety of services that have recently been offered as part of the ACLF-funded 'Feeling Good' initiative.

What the centre offers

A wide range of projects has been delivered through the coordinated efforts of the team at Keighley Healthy Living Centre. Some projects were based at the Centre itself, but others were based within various communities, in people's homes, in schools and on allotments. Part of the Centre's work focuses on learning for health, and a range of course were offered as part of the Adult and Community Learning Fund, including:

- Gardening for Health Project
- Feeling Good at the Roshni Ghar (centre of light) – a creative, confidence-building and English skills programme
- Health and exercise
- Parenting programmes.

A total of 165 participants enrolled on various courses of the Feeling Good initiative. Taster days coordinated through the Centre included a variety of short courses ranging from Art Attack through alternative therapies to Helping Your Child at School. An International Women's Day event organised by local residents in 2001 attracted 300 people.

It becomes apparent from talking to Jill and Hawarun that the success of the Feeling Good initiative is based on a range of factors – all of which relate to an intimate knowledge of the nature of the learners for whom the Centre provides educational services. This knowledge comes from desire, dedication and passion for learning on the part of the staff. From a practical point of view, the Centre recognises the importance of harnessing the skills, talents and knowledge of local residents and of getting into the community through a variety of outreach techniques. All techniques directly involve, or need the support of, people with intimate knowledge of the cultural, religious and social issues – particularly with reference to the Bangladeshi and Pakistani communities. Jill informed me that:

The ethnic minority community in Keighley is strongly Islamic, closely knit and concentrated in certain streets in the town. As a result, publicity about what we do is largely word of mouth, and this is very effective. It is due to the skills of development workers at the KHLN that our education programme has become widely known, and we understand that the community feels that there has been a positive response to their needs. Continued outreach work throughout the programme is essential. It encourages regular attendance and keeps the profile of what we do high in the community.

Word-of-mouth publicity is particularly important in Keighley, because a significant number of people within the Asian community have low levels of literacy and because the better equipped are not used to receiving information – for example, about courses – in writing. Hawarun's role as community outreach worker has been invaluable in this process, because she goes into various areas and spreads the word about the value of the work of the KHLN.

HAWARUN HUSSAIN (PROJECT WORKER) AND JILL KIBBLE (MANAGER, KHLC)

The project has two development workers; one is an older Pakistani woman who, through an intimate knowledge of her community, identified the need for the 50+ Fit Group that the KHLN coordinates. Most of the courses, tasters and drop-in opportunities offered through the KHLN are area based: staff find this works best. A few years ago, discussion focussed on setting up a healthy living centre centrally based in Keighley, but the general feeling then, as now, was that this would not work for Keighley. As Jill states:

It's not about a building; it's about making use of locally based facilities and providing services from within them, and it's not about creating additional facilities when those that already exist are under-utilised.

What KHLN offers is about working with local communities in a number of ways. Providing courses and so on for the benefit of various groups – from young Asian men to people over 50 years old – and working with local people with the skills and knowledge to reach out into the community. These people know the community and what the community's issues; they are role models and have a personal investment in making sure what they do works.

This knowledge is particularly important when services are offered to learners who have not previously attended formal courses – and most of those who attended various courses as part of the Feeling Good initiative have not. People who previously had attended mainstream English for Speakers of Other Languages classes had reported that these were often unable to meet their needs, particularly if they were offered from large formal colleges. These can be particularly daunting places and can present a huge challenge for the learner – even getting to the college can be a challenge if the learner has only a basic grasp of English. This, explains Hawarun, is one of the reasons why people in the Asian community rely on taxis: many taxi drivers are Asian, so that an Asian customer with minimal English can easily direct the driver to the destination. Without English, explaining your destination to a bus driver or using a train is daunting!

For this reason, the Feeling Good initiative offers practical courses – the initiative is not about teaching English as an end in itself, but is more about exploring the use of English in real-life situations and viewing it as a means to a practical end. Courses are delivered predominantly in English and are designed to build oral confidence. All the content is student-centred and developed through negotiation with learners. The content and delivery is often developed after taster courses or short, directed programmes that are designed to build and inform learners about the range of opportunities available.

The Asian Women's Project and neighbourhood renewal

The KNLN ran an eight-week organic gardening programme in English. This demonstrates the multi-pronged approach that tutors take to adult and community learning. First, the course provided English support as well as introducing the women to a new range of words that enabled them to shop for vegetables and to use in their cooking. One of the target groups for this course was older (mainly age 50+) Bangladeshi women, and it was very successful in its aims. The incidence of diabetes and heart disease are relatively high within the Asian community, and the not-so-hidden agenda was to give learners a health focus and explore how diet and what we eat has a direct bearing on health. Hawarun informed me that one of her biggest challenges was trying to get women to consider using an alternative to ghee as their cooking oil – it is a challenge she is still working on.

Exercise was also part of the course for the older women, as was work around psychological well-being, because the incidence of psychological problems amongst Asian women is disproportionately high; this relates particularly to the isolation they experience because of their lack of English. Jill acknowledges this and notes that one of the most important issues with regard to community health relates to where people live and the absolute relation between belonging and health. In this sense, much of the KHLN's work is linked directly to neighbourhood renewal, because it enables local people to realise their full potential through 'empowering to participate'. This is done in a very fundamental way – through their acquisition and confident application of the English language.

Neighbourhood renewal

People in Keighley benefit from the accumulation of social capital – gained through various learning opportunities delivered from a variety of locations – and a greater understanding of issues of health and health promotion. Jill explains:

> **Neighbourhood renewal is vitally important, for us it's about empowering people who are otherwise isolated. We work with a lot of people who have no English. We do the**

gardening work, but we also help people with their English through an oracy project. We also facilitate services with partner organisations for victims of domestic violence as well as legal and housing advice surgeries. Most of all, we are very much a network, and partnership working is central to our methodology; that is why we encourage organisations to offer similar services, particularly through our work with the college and the WEA [Workers' Educational Association].

The beauty of the gardening project is that it is so positive for health in terms of exercise and what people take home for the family to eat. A lot of people in the Asian community tend to eat fruit and greens that are imported – and expensive. The gardening project encourages women to use cheaper alternatives. The women also take a pride in their allotments – so much so, that the KHLN is looking at ways of extending the existing allotments and is looking for additional allotments.

Having an identity in the community

Hawarun explained that many women in the Asian community do not have their own individual identity within the community. I wondered how different this is to the experience of many women in white communities, but Hawarun explained further:

When they are born, they are someone's daughter; when they marry, they become someone's wife; and then when they have children, they become someone's mother. They have no individual identity, and this affects the way people see themselves and their ability to participate.

Add to this the geographical isolation and the isolation women experience through not speaking English, and it is obvious how innovative and effective is the work of the KHLN.

The success of the Asian community

The Asian community in Keighley is successful in a range of ways – despite its perception as insular. The women who participate in the courses run through the KHLN completely dispel the stereotyped idea of timid, non-participatory, Asian woman! In fact Asian women have offered their services to the KHLN in a variety of ways – as volunteers, mentors and role models and as skilled linguists and concerned parents.

Keighley's Asian communities have not been impressed by government initiatives. As Hawarun points out, these initiatives make too many assumptions about the way people live. For example, Sure Start can seem patronising to parents who are already positive and do an excellent job of bringing up their children, while Community Wardens could cause rifts in Asian communities and discourage efforts, such as keeping an eye on children playing in the streets, that are already in practice.

Unsurprisingly, after their time on a KHLN course, a significant number of women come back to sample something new. Many women need support over a long period of time. The KHLN certainly does not expect women to jump straight into accredited courses – as Jill explains:

There is nothing wrong with horizontal progression; people do a whole range of sideways moves and even take steps backwards or stop for short periods of time.

Some people go onto greater and higher things. An older learner with a disabled husband, who had been a volunteer at Roshni Ghar, recently enrolled on a City and Guilds 7303 course (to gain a qualification in adult teaching) and passed with flying colours. This is the greatest aspect of neighbourhood renewal for tutors and learners at the KHLC. Work is carried out with people who know the community. People who take advantage of courses often come back as volunteers and then, like Hawarun, they go on to play a significant role in making a difference further afield.

Keighley Healthy Living Centre provides an inspirational and organic way to meet the needs of people from a very specific community by linking a range of skills, including language acquisition, cooking, growing vegetables, healthy eating and exercise. Jill, Hawarun and their colleagues intentionally designed their services in this way, so they meet the needs of 'whole' individuals and equip them with the tools they need to participate actively and make a difference in their own lives, as well as those of their families and communities.

Keighley
Healthy
Living
Nework

-3-

WOMEN: LEARNING THE SKILLS FOR ACTIVE ENGAGEMENT

WILLOW WOMEN'S CENTRE
Women into leisure, life or work

❝ Not enough is done to provide 'first-rung' provision that can help people with low self-confidence or motivation to take the first steps back into learning. Such provision can take any number of forms – examples might include first aid, childcare or local history. What is important is that it engages local people's interests and helps them to see how learning might be relevant to them.

POLICY ACTION TEAM 2 – SKILLS ❞

Willow
Women's
Centre

KINGSTON UPON HULL

TAKE A LOOK AT HULL'S 'VIRTUAL HULL' WEBSITE (www.virtual-hull.com) and you will learn that the City Centre Hull partnership is Hull's leading strategic body for city centre affairs. It is a pioneering company funded by Hull Cityventure, Kingston upon Hull City Council and the city's business community. The partnership's vision is of a city centre that is a safe, vibrant and attractive place in which to live, work, visit and invest. Hull is the major centre of the Humber region and has a travel-to-work population of close to 450,000.

Regeneration chiefs expect Hull to benefit from closer ties with Europe in the future because of its strategic position on the E20 trade route. This route links the UK and Ireland with Northern Europe and makes the city, with its port, a natural commercial and industrial location.

Hull was one of the first authorities to introduce radical changes to its local government system. With the aim of generating greater public participation where possible, all decisions are devolved to the city's seven area committees, which are coupled with neighbourhood forums that allow issues to be raised at the grassroots level.

The streamlined system of local democracy is also designed to enhance the public and private partnerships' campaign to get Hull into the top ten cities in the UK. Through a range of economic, educational and community initiatives, Kingston upon Hull City Council is supporting efforts to get Hull recognised as one of the UK's key locations.

Traditionally, Hull relied heavily on the fishing industry, but in the 1980s, Britain joined the European Economic Community and had to adhere to strict fishing restrictions and regulations. Many of the local factories were linked to the fishing industry because they processed fish, and additional subsidiary industries and services – such as ships' chandlers – supported the fleets of North Sea trawlers that regularly sailed along the River Humber. Now the fishing industry

SHARON GAMBLE (WILLOW TRAINING CO-ORDINATOR) IN ACTION

and associated services have all gone, and major urban renewal, including property and business developments, has occurred, along with the building of major road networks. The Hull by-pass is a spectacular road that runs under the impressive Humber suspension bridge and alongside the Humber Estuary, passes the old docks and new commerce area, and circles the town centre. The North Sea Ferries still operate, and it is possible to travel from Hull to Amsterdam, Rotterdam and Zeebrugge.

Cultural diversity

Although Hull was the home of the great slavery abolitionist William Willberforce (who left the people of Hull an impressive museum), in terms of cultural diversity the city has no real black community. It has a very small Asian community and a small number of asylum-seekers – who come mainly from Eastern Europe, but also from East Africa.

Hull has a number of social issues and, in some senses, is like many other cities. I was informed that:

> **There are drug dealers who openly deal on some estates, needles to be found in telephone boxes, alcoholics on the streets, but things are getting better.**

WILLOW WOMEN'S CENTRE

The WILLOW women's centre is an independent registered charity set up to provide activities and services for women living in the Hull area. WILLOW stands for Women Into Leisure, Life or Work, and the meaning of this acronym really does sum up the centre. It is a refuge in some ways, it is a place for women to experiment and learn in other ways, and finally it is a place for women to discover more about themselves and the social relationships they have.

Hull benefits from SRB round 6 funding. North Hull, the area adjacent to the area in which the WILLOW women's centre is found, receives SRB round 4 funding. Margaret MacDonald, centre administrator for WILLOW, tells me a familiar story:

Funding is averaged out, so we miss out because we're in the University Ward; there is some affluence around here, but also a couple of estates are in the area – North Hull Estate as well as Orchard Park – and there is a lot of poverty and social problems on these estates.

WILLOW aims to broaden the outlook of and opportunities for women living in the area by boosting their self-confidence and enabling them to reach their full potential. To achieve this, the centre aims to:

- provide a safe, caring and friendly environment
- enable women to meet other women
- further women's education outside of the context of the formal classroom
- provide affordable, high-quality childcare for women while they use the centre
- represent the interests of local women
- encourage women to participate in the running of the centre
- provide opportunities for voluntary work
- enable women to make a useful contribution to their communi

The centre's day-to-day work is carried out by a team of paid workers and volunteers, and it is managed by a committee of local women. I met with Margaret MacDonald, part-time worker (three paid hours a week plus many hours of volunteering), and Jacquie Newman, project administrator, to find out more about the work of WILLOW. On the day I went to the centre, several women were learning with their children and with the training coordinator, Sharon Gamble, about Egypt: how to make a mummy, to draw hieroglyphics onto cartouches and to design, cut and paint broad collars for mummies.

Many of the women WILLOW caters for come from very traditional backgrounds in which the man is the main breadwinner. I was informed that, even if the family is on social security, the man considers himself to be the breadwinner – he will be the main claimant. In many instances, the woman will be a 'non-person' – not even a claimant in her own right and not known or recognised by 'the system'. In this way, many women are brainwashed into accepting an inferior and limited place within the household and within the community. Margaret informed me that:

We have a woman doing a degree with us and her husband did everything that he could to stop this. He prevented her from doing her homework and always made sure that he was not available to look after the kids; this put tremendous pressure on her and it's a sign of her sheer will and determination that she succeeded – despite her husband!

WILLOW's policy is that men are not allowed in the centre, except in exceptional circumstances. For example, a male tutor delivers the City and Guilds 7307 course (a practical qualification for those who wish to become teachers) that the centre offers. He comes into the building through a different entrance to the women; this arrangement is born out of necessity and relates directly to the fact that many women have experienced domestic violence and are in the complicated process of taking very small steps back to normality. The presence of a man could, for some women, lead to a series of large backward steps towards uncertainty and depression. Some health and safety and building work has also been performed by men – as has some of the art; the caretaker is a man, but he does most of his work when no women are in the centre.

In recent years, the centre has gone from strength to strength, offering an increasing range of learning opportunities for women – from Egyptology through basic counselling to Internet for Beginners. This has been made possible through a committed team of staff, an active management committee, a regular group of enthusiastic volunteers and the use of rooms in the Hall Road Youth Centre. Debbie Bainbridge, chairperson of WILLOW, explained that the organisation is able to offer an extended range of courses because of its approach to partnership working, particularly with Hull College and the Community Learning Service.

In addition, the centre has recently secured financial support from the Community Fund. This has enabled it to provide an extended service not only in terms of the wide variety of courses described, but also in terms of longer opening hours: the centre opens with crèche facilities in the early evening – a significant departure from its previous 9.00 am–3.00 pm opening hours – to extend its reach. As Sharon noted, 'the community fund has been the backbone

FAMILY LEARNING AND EGYPTOLOGY

of our funding for the past three years; the new project will give us another three years to help, train and support the women in the local area'.

Between 2001 and 2002, WILLOW increased student numbers by over 150 per term. It achieved this by increasing course availability and diversity and by working closely with local women and educational partners to ensure that the choice of courses offered was user-led.

WILLOW recently bid for funding from the Learning and Skills Council to support family learning. The success of this bid will be known within three months of the application. WILLOW recently received funding from the Home Office for the Volunteers in Practice (VIP) project – a teaching and recruitment programme.

PARTNERSHIP WORKING

Partnership is very important to the WILLOW centre. As Jacquie and Margaret informed me, 'it ensures that you avoid duplication and that you take a strategic approach to what you deliver'; it gives an informed overview of what's needed and what learners are requesting. Partnerships can inform WILLOW's strategy and approach to planning.

> **Partnerships with the voluntary sector and educational providers have proved the point that working together brings rewards. Multi-agency partnerships can be seen as infeasible and are often overlooked in the development of voluntary organisations. WILLOW has shown that this benefits small organisations, helping to contribute to capacity-building [for] both local organisations and the local community as a whole. (WILLOW Annual Report 2001–2002)**

First Steps Group

One of the many innovative services provided through WILLOW is the First Steps Group, which is run by a steering group of women from the centre. The Group's main aim is to get very vulnerable women – usually those with mental illnesses, alcoholism or low self-esteem – into the centre. These women often come to the centre through doctors' referrals and counselling services, and they can also join in with the Group by talking to other women on the telephone. Margaret explained:

> **It takes time to get some women to engage, and this causes a problem with funders. They are more than just bums on seats: just to get someone to walk through the door is a challenge. We have some women who have stood outside on a number of occasions not having the confidence to come in – now we can't get shut of half of them. We take anyone [who] for any reason…can't necessarily go into regular groups because they are not ready for traditional learning routes – and we're talking mainly about minor mental illnesses. These women come from all over the city. We all have the same role but I [Margaret] get paid for three hours a week.**

The group has been going for just over a year and about 30 women have been members. Women don't have to give their names – some can't write, and the group is keen not to frighten women away.

After taking their first tiny steps into the First Steps Group, most women have moved onto various courses at WILLOW. One woman who was in an abusive relationship started to come to the centre when her relationship broke up; now she is serving on the First Step Steering Committee after taking several courses through WILLOW.

Margaret came to the centre in 1997 with her own problems. She had undergone a breakdown and has no problem telling people about this, because it's one of the many strategies she uses to get close to her client group. She can empathise with them, as well as act as a role model. She knows what they've experienced, and she is living proof that it is possible to succeed with support and understanding – no matter what kind of problem a woman has had in her past.

Margaret believes that WILLOW's work is about neighbourhood renewal. She explained:

> **We have women going to college, into paid employment. They have more pride in themselves and in their area. Another woman has gone on to become a teacher having recently completed her teacher training. She works with disabled adults.**

Capacity-building

Jacquie came to the centre in 1995 after she moved onto neighbouring estate. She came in for reflexology, and everything progressed from there. First, she went on a women's studies course, which is something that she had always been interested in. This led her to go back to college to take GCSEs in English and Maths. From there, she progressed onto computer courses and then became a volunteer on WILLOW's management committee. In September 2000, she was offered the job of administrator. Jacquie explains, 'This is quite a complicated role, and one that has developed as the organisation has grown and developed.' She is a prime example of why it's important for people who have used services, been on training courses and worked as volunteers to come back to provide those services – a sort of recycling. Jacquie says that she has a thirst for learning, and as a parent of four children she has to juggle her time and commitments.

The nature of WILLOW's work and issues of confidentiality mean that:

It is very hard for us to monitor women once they have gone on from here, but we know that they do go to university, college and into employment. We do build up the capacity of women through our centre and offer various progression routes through WILLOW.

Empowering women

Women are encouraged to take advantage of our courses, which are about assertion and handing stress – they can be accredited for these. Some women see the centre as a refuge from the outside world – it's safe, it's friendly, the learning that we offer is non-traditional and, as women, we appreciate that our women have additional responsibilities such as childcare.

In terms of 'added value', as well as providing free crèche services, WILLOW also provides free counselling. Four counsellors operate from the Centre. Women who are taking the diploma course in counselling at Hull University are offered free placements, provide hour-long sessions and have three clients each. The service is totally confidential. Clients are referred by doctors and community nurses. Some clients are already on courses and take advantage of the counselling service, but for most women, counselling opens the door for them to take advantage of other services and courses.

WILLOW also provides out-of-school activities during the school holidays; these include Pamper Days, which enable mothers who have been challenged by their children over the six weeks of summer holidays to wind down and have a little space. Women can make use of nail art facilities, reflexology and 'Customise Crazy' (women bring in and customise their own clothes). WILLOW also has a summer spectacular in September: a magic show is put on for children, bouncy castles are available and a big party is held in the garden of the former primary school that WILLOW uses courtesy (and free of charge) of one of its many partners – the Local Education Authority.

WILLOW is more than a women's refuge or a family-learning centre; it has elements of both, and more. It is a place where women can be themselves in a secure learning environment and with other women who have had similar experiences and can empathise. WILLOW is not about cocooning women in a soft cuddly environment though, because staff recognise that there is a world beyond the safe haven of WILLOW. It is a world that the women should participate in because they have so much to offer – skills and abilities they have always had and new knowledge acquired through the centre.

CALDERDALE WELL WOMAN CENTRE
Basic skills and opportunities for women

‘In some areas, there are deep-seated cultural attitudes which lead people to discount the benefits of learning. Over time, such attitudes can lead to a culture which lacks enterprise and appreciation of the potential of enterprise.’

POLICY ACTION TEAM 2 – SKILLS

Calderdale
Well Woman
Centre

CALDERDALE WELL WOMAN CENTRE is located in one of the smaller metropolitan districts. Halifax, Calderdale's largest town, accounts for almost half of the district's population of 197,000. It is a varied geographical area, with some rural and urban communities, characterised by terraced housing. Manufacturing accounts for almost one-third of local employment – this far exceeds the national average of 18 per cent – and the Halifax Building Society is a major employer. Five per cent of the population is Asian in origin – primarily from Pakistan – and mainly resides in one area of Halifax. This community requires specific educational services, such as support in learning English. To meet the specific needs of different communities, the Centre has a number of extended arms, including area-based projects that operate on an outreach basis, as well as its central base in Halifax.

The furthermost community served by the project is Mixenden, which is about four miles outside Halifax. Mixenden is a very disadvantaged community, with few education services and historically poor take-up of the services that do exist. Calderdale is a very traditional area that historically relied on the textile industry for most of its employment. Many women who take advantage of the first-step provision offered by the Calderdale Well Woman Centre are carers of small children. The various communities to which such women belong usually do not expect that they will ever do anything else. Clare Jones, project coordinator, explains:

Many people have lived in the same geographically confined communities all their lives; sometimes these only consist of a few streets, but there is a strong identity and association with these areas with very little mobility and traditional and often patriarchal attitudes.

THE WOMEN'S LEARNING PROJECT

The Women's Learning Project aimed to offer accessible learning activities to women who were not able to access other forms of learning because of reasons such as mental health problems, the effects of domestic violence or learning difficulties. Confidence and communication skills were identified as basic skill requirements for the women involved, and all learning activities share the same aim of building confidence and improving social skills.

West Central Halifax has a large Asian community, but when the Women's Learning Project first opened in 1999, t was clear that women from this community were not taking advantage of the services on offer. This led to the development of outreach strategies and the concentration of services around familiar bases, such as the St Augustine's Family Centre. The successful provision and take-up of services from this Centre was made possible by the development of partnerships and the use of existing knowledge about minority communities. The Workers' Educational Association, for example, had traditionally had good contacts and relationships with the Pakistani community, and it was this relationship that led to the successful development of programmes at the St Augustine's Family Centre and the training and employment of Asian tutors.

During the life of the project, strong links were built with voluntary and statutory organisations, including the Domestic Violence Support Project, Women's Aid, the Probation Service, Community Mental Health teams and Care in the Community teams. Links were also developed with Calderdale College and, in particular, Local Learning and Pecket Well Community College.

WOMEN OF ALL AGES USE THE CENTRE

Project beneficiaries and publicity

The target group for the project was women who encounter barriers to accessing learning in more formal settings. Clare and her colleagues were also keen to attract women who were unemployed and previously had not taken part in adult education. Participants typically had low self-esteem, and most had come to know about the Project from other support agencies linked to the Calderdale Well Woman Centre. Project information and course details were regularly mailed to voluntary and statutory sector groups, and the Project and its courses also featured regularly in the Calderdale Voluntary Action newsletters. Flyers were distributed to health centres, libraries and community centres. Confidence-building courses for women were advertised in the Adult and Community Learning Guide and on the Learningline.

Considerable amounts of time were spent discussing the project with the Careers Service, Local Learning and Student Support Services at Calderdale College. As the project developed, participants made others aware of courses and activities themselves – by word of mouth and by leafleting local shops and facilities. Tutors attended group meetings at Women's Aid and the Domestic Violence Support Project to discuss courses and the informal and flexible approach to learning that was provided.

Adult and community learning

The Project generally offered non-accredited courses to meet the immediate needs of women in their daily lives. Most participants consistently cited confidence building as essential for improving their quality of life. All courses were unique, were tailored to meet the individual needs of the women and were adjusted continually to ensure that they met the needs of each learning group. The team of tutors was selected specifically for their sensitivity and their understanding of the likely issues, fears and concerns for women learners participating for the first time.

A personal approach was adopted, and learners were encouraged to use real-life situations to practice new skills. For example, one learner who had serious physical disabilities developed the assertiveness and communication skills needed to negotiate successfully with her family and Social Services to arrange changes to her living situation – an issue that had caused her personal distress for many months. Other women practised communicating with services and agencies, including solicitors, benefit advisers and doctors. Learners were encouraged to discover for themselves the positive experience and results of learning.

Calderdale Well Woman Centre

Learning took place in small, friendly and relaxed groups that offered women the opportunity to develop social contacts and to access the range of support services offered at the Centre and elsewhere in the community. Partners on the Project believed that this approach would put women in good stead to move onto more formal and structured courses and to start the long journey that would lead to greater levels of participation in their communities.

Participants of activities and programmes provided by the Calderdale Well Woman Centre quickly developed a variety of skills, including stress management, assertiveness and speaking with confidence. They achieved personal goals, while trying out new things, such as meeting new people and working together as a group. Approximately half of all learners continued with further learning when their course had ended – either through further courses offered by the Centre, part-time college courses or Worker's Educational Association (WEA)-accredited courses.

Courses offered

The Project offered short courses and occasional events, which were usually based at the Centre, but could also be offered at two other areas of particular deprivation within Halifax. Most courses ran for a minimum of three weeks and a maximum of ten weeks, and they included one two-hour session each week. Childcare was made available for all courses, and transport costs were offered on a discretionary basis. The courses offered included:

- Basic Skills and Confidence Building
- Rights and Opportunities for Women
- Self-development through Drama
- Confidence through Creativity
- Stress Management
- Creating Your Own Destiny
- Well Women Learning Groups.

A typical, ten-session course on confidence building would begin with an introductory session, during which each learner would be encouraged to explain their own aims for the course and how they hoped this would improve their quality of life. In this first session, the group would develop an identity through icebreaking exercises and the negotiation of ground rules. Tutors would then use learner feedback to inform the delivery and content of all further sessions. Over the following weeks, women worked in small groups to explore the fundamentals of communication and to practice listening skills and assertiveness techniques. Creative sessions enabled learners to develop self-awareness through collages and imagery. Later sessions included a focus on personal goals, options for the future and action planning.

The Centre's Volunteer Programme ran every six months. It offered Level 2 accreditation through the West and North Yorkshire Open College Network in the following units:

- Centre Awareness and the Volunteer Role

- Health Awareness and Signposting

- Good Practice for Women's Issues.

The style of delivery was intentionally interactive, so as to empower women to contribute and have confidence in their own opinions. Each course started by asking all learners to agree a set of guidelines that would ensure the course remained comfortable and effective for all participants. The next group decision was an inclusive list of the aims of the course; this opened up the various possibilities of learning and acted as a personal evaluation tool. Feedback on an informal and personal level was sought often throughout each course, and the content was modified as a result. Although the ten-week confidence-building course ran on four occasions, each course was very different with respect to the teaching methods and course materials used, so as to meet the specific needs of each group. All tutors quickly developed a similar delivery style that generally used handouts only to circulate information generated by the group during the previous week.

Written information was introduced verbally and supported the learning participants achieved through experience. Experimental forms of learning included hands-on experience where appropriate, creative and practical activities designed by tutors and role playing of real and imagined situations. Small-group work facilitated the development of confidence, with even the most anxious women eventually able to be spokesperson for their small group – a real achievement given the backgrounds and experiences of some women who regularly came to the Centre.

The Centre allowed learners to develop confidence and become aware of their value as group members. Many groups expressed their appreciation towards each other, for example by sharing cards at the end of the course. Participants found that they could enjoy different types of relationship outside the home – a discovery that acted as a crucial incentive for the social and educational participation of many isolated women. This was reflected in the comments of women, which revealed how, in some instances, their experiences at the Centre had been life changing, had enabled them to think outside their immediate families and had allowed them to create a fuller picture of who they were, what their community meant to them and their potential within that community.

Assessing success

The Project developed a variety of evaluation tools to capture the 'soft outcomes' that made significant differences to the lives of learners. The Project collected information from learners on the usefulness and relevance of each course and activity as well as the participants enjoyment of the course and areas in which they were dissatisfied. Learners were also encouraged to make suggestions as to how the courses on offer could be improved.

Information was also gathered from tutors and mentors about the effectiveness of each session and the extent to which they had met their objectives. This needed a consideration of attendance figures, recording and evaluation of delivery methods, critical review of the available learning materials and environmental factors, and identification of the needs and problems experienced by groups and individuals.

Evaluation methods included:

- end of topic and end of course evaluation sheets

- end of topic tutor and mentor evaluation sheets

- ongoing informal feedback from tutors, learners and referral and support projects

WORKING TOGETHER ACROSS AGE AND CULTURAL DIFFERENCES

Calderdale Well Woman Centre

- questionnaires

- original ways of encouraging independent comments from learners – for example, speech bubbles, boxes and pointers (paper shapes for comments referring to likes and dislikes) and two hands for likes and dislikes.

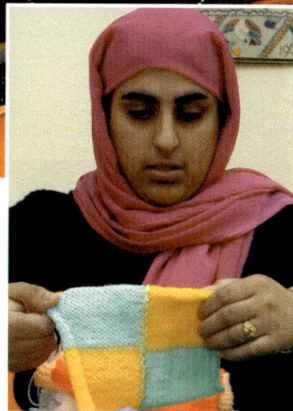

Neighbourhood renewal

The Project has contributed to neighbourhood renewal in three particular areas – Halifax Centre, West Central Halifax and Mixenden – and in different ways in each area. In Halifax Centre, women who had been isolated and were not able to participate in social or community activities have formed new social networks and are helping and supporting each other. This has been of particular benefit to single mothers and women suffering from depression and anxiety. In Mixenden, women have used confidence-building skills to engage in local community initiatives, including volunteering and joining the management committee of the Mixenden Parents Resource Centre.

In West Central Halifax, the project has provided an opportunity for cultural sharing and the building of trust between white and Asian women of different ages. The group members are proud of the ethnic and cultural mix of the group and speak openly of its success and value to church groups and other community groups. Overall, the project has enabled marginalised women to engage in their communities and to develop a love of learning and participation.

Taking things forward

Calderdale Well Women Centre ran its initial courses with support from the ACLF, and it has been eager to keep things going and to build on the solid foundation already laid down for the women of Halifax and the surrounding area. The Centre was successful in a subsequent bid for ACLF that will support the development of focus groups. Clare explains:

> **We have been able to keep things going, and groups have largely run themselves, with women coming back to the centre for meetings and to keep the social contact going. We have had some support from the local council towards capacity building and now from the Adult and Community Learning Fund to establish focus groups. These will help to widen participation and lead to further engagement, particularly of women from isolated groups.**

The further development of the work in Calderdale Valley will ensure that the educational services provided are right for the women in the area. It also will enable Clare and her colleagues to work with women who have not yet sampled the Centre's courses, such as women from areas like Todmorden – a quiet, rural and detached community 16 miles from Halifax centre.

Clare is committed to continued partnership working and to collecting knowledge and information on the nature and needs of various local communities. Clare is confident that information and partnership – coupled with the views and perspective of women in the focus groups – will ensure that the services and courses Calderdale Well Woman Centre offers continue to become better and more relevant. The Centre should produce greater levels of community involvement and empowerment of women in a very traditional area of the country.

-4-

BASELINE
RESEARCH,
PROVIDING THE
RIGHT LEARNING
OPPORTUNITIES

Growing communities

'The problems facing deprived neighbourhoods are multi-faceted and not joined up. A combination of public, private, voluntary and community sector effort is needed to address them. The need to join up is particularly strong at the local (i.e. local authority) level. It is at this level that many core public services do their operational planning, and at which many decisions about allocation of resources are made.'

POLICY ACTION TEAM 17 – JOINING IT UP LOCALLY

Norwich
City
Council

NORWICH

NORWICH IS THE ONLY CITY IN NORFOLK and the largest urban area in the Eastern region of England. On the face of it, Norwich is affluent and prosperous; its city centre is full of character and features a range of historic buildings, a castle and two cathedrals. With a population of about 126,000, Norwich has a buoyant economy and a lot of business investment. Around 250,000 people live in Norwich's 'travel-to-work area', unemployment currently stands at 4.3 per cent in the city itself (2.2 per cent in the city and travel-to-work area) and 80 per cent of employed people work in service industries.

Despite outward appearances, Norwich is the second most deprived area in the Eastern region. Twenty-five per cent of the adult population of Norwich have no formal qualifications, an estimated 30 per cent lack Level 2 basic skills in numeracy and literacy and 34 per cent have never engaged in formal learning since leaving school. In addition, although communities in many deprived areas of the country have a strong sense of self-help and a history of community activism, Norwich has little history or tradition in this respect. It was in part recognition of this fact that a range of initiatives to develop active citizens and a community-led Learning City were started in Norwich.

DEVELOPING A COMMUNITY-LED LEARNING CITY

The path for developing a community-led Learning City started in 1995, when Norwich City Council worked with local communities, through the Community Power initiative, to develop 12 community-based Area Forums. The Forums involve democratically elected people and aim to involve local people in making decisions about their communities and their own lives. The Learning City Initiative, which started at the same time, aims to create a culture of lifelong learning.

Learning City Initiative

The key drivers of the Learning City Initiative are the low level of educational attainment and poor skills base of residents of Norwich and their impact on the residents' learning potential and the competitiveness of Norwich businesses. Many people from Norwich are not benefiting currently from the city's economic successes, and a significant proportion is excluded economically. At the same time, the competitiveness of the Norwich business base is restricted to some extent by the skills and aspirations of the workforce and the potential workforce. The position is masked to a degree by the local economy drawing in over 50,000 commuters from the surrounding, more affluent districts.

The work of the Learning City initiative includes taking steps to make people aware of training and employment opportunities. The initiative offers taster and 'bite-sized' training and learning opportunities as well as advice and guidance. All of these services have been provided for, and increasingly with, the people of Norwich, through a range of initiatives and support services that have meant the development of partnerships and the need for a strategic mode of operation to maximise impact.

The Learning City initiative adds value to the range of statutory provision and learning

ACTIVE AND VISIBLE

initiatives by targeting the need for community learning, in particular 'first-rung' learning. This is often an informal, community-based activity that focuses on engaging hard-to-reach individuals and groups in learning and helping them to progress into mainstream learning, where appropriate.

Norwich Learning City Group

The Norwich Learning City Group is taking the lead on developing the community-led Learning City. The Group has recently researched baseline data and analysed service provision and has started to identify local needs for each of the Area Forum districts. This work is being integrated into area community plans to encourage uptake of community learning.

I met with a range of partners in the City Council offices, Norwich City Council's European and Economic Development Unit, Norwich City College and Norwich Adult Education Service to find out about the Learning City – its aims, challenges and future developments – and, in particular, about how the Group is trying to engage community groups.

The Group works to create a 'bottom-up' approach to learning and to develop genuine partnerships between learning providers and local communities, focusing on:

- supporting local communities to identify and articulate their learning needs, to secure appropriate community-based provision and to integrate activity into the community planning process

- securing resources to increase considerably the availability community-based and community-led learning

- helping local learning providers work more effectively with and for local communities

- helping local communities to develop the capacity to meet some of their own learning needs

- ensuring that Learning City activities are integrated with and support other social and economic policy agendas and initiatives in Norwich.

The Group is aware that learning can transform people's lives. The creation of a culture of life-long learning has a positive impact on many social and economic policy areas, including economic, community and cultural development, and health and community safety. Most importantly, it opens doors for personal growth and fulfilment.

Norwich Learning City Group has managed a number of initiatives that have paved the way for the development of Community Learning Action Plans. These include an area-profiling research exercise to establish the local population's skills and education attainment levels, to map the existing community-based learning infrastructure and to identify perceived needs and barriers to learning as well as an initiative to encourage community participation through marketing activities such as festivals and events, Learning City involvement in local community events and articles in the Learning City News, which has a circulation of 12,000.

Resourcing community learning action planning

Priorities identified through action plans have to be resourced and supported in a range of ways. Norwich Learning City Group has coordinated a range of initiatives and support services to ensure that this happens. Recent developments include:

- Refocusing of the Learning City SRB development officer's role by scaling down Learning Festival activities to create time and resources to support the development of Community Learning Action Plans in six Area Forums. The other six Forums are to be supported by a development officer, and funding has been secured through the Learning and Skills Council.

- Development of the Learning City Community Projects Fund, which will support

Community Learning Action Plans with projects to build community capacity and will respond to local needs identified by the Action Plans.

■ Learning City On-Line: development of a community-based information and communications technology learning infrastructure across the city using £680,000 from the successful bid to UK On-Line and the National Lottery and £1.5 million from Match Funding.

Developing the community development skills of learning providers

Capacity building and gearing people to participate and decide the direction for Norwich as a community-led Learning City has to take place on a number of fronts. Training and support also has to be given by locally based learning providers.

Norwich Learning City Group recognises that, although the capacity to participate within learning partnerships has to be developed in local residents, the capacity also has to be grown in service providers. This is why the Norwich Learning City Group organised a staff development seminar 'Working in and with local communities' in February 2002. This seminar was targeted at public, voluntary, community and private sector organisations that deliver community-based learning.

The results of the Learning City Group's research with providers and participants in community learning in 2001 were presented at the seminar. The research identified best practice and highlighted staff development needs. The seminar also kick-started an activity aimed at addressing the development needs of policy-makers and bid-writers from learning providers and community-based staff who deliver community learning.

Norwich Learning City Network

An additional part of the process of creating Community Learning Action Plans involves networking at a grassroots level. The Norwich Learning City Group set up the Norwich Learning City Network to combine across various sectors, such as health, community safety, community development, and youth and community. The Network aims to:

■ engage people working at a grassroots level in the lifelong learning agenda

■ increase community and provider understanding of local needs

■ improve two-way dialogue about local needs and the appropriateness of provision between local communities and learning providers (across the sectors)

■ increase the amount of community learning by encouraging a wider range of agencies to include learning elements in their community provision

■ join up the agendas of local providers – for example, between health, community safety and learning projects

■ encourage a wider range of organisations to access Learning City SRB funding.

Benefits for learning providers include:

■ availability of information to help channel mainstream funding from local providers into community needs and community-based programmes

COMMUNITY SELF-DETERMINATION

▪ opportunities to discuss local needs with communities to facilitate community-led or bottom-up development and management of community learning activities

▪ leverage, through better evidence of local needs and demands, to acquire additional resources and to underpin provider-led bids for funding and opportunities for community-led funding bids.

COMMUNITY SELF-DETERMINATION

I asked when Norwich would know that it has successfully developed a community-led Learning City. The overwhelming response to this question was exactly what I had expected after spending an afternoon with a group of committed optimists, 'It's an ongoing ambition; we are aiming for cultural change. To create a culture of lifelong learning may take a generation or more'. A good indicator, however, will be a developed and maturing area-based system of local democracy – a system in which the people of Norwich are confident, informed and able to make decisions about their futures and the future of their city, as they become more active citizens.

REDDITCH ALLEARN
Redditch ALLearn
Partnership

These [poor] communities exist right across the country, north and south, rural and urban. They may be cut off on the edge of cities, or close to the city centre and wealthy suburbs. They may be high-rise council estates, or streets of private rented or even owner-occupied homes.

A NEW COMMITMENT TO NEIGHBOURHOOD RENEWAL –

NATIONAL STRATEGY ACTION PLAN, 2001

REDDITCH WAS VERY MUCH A MARKET TOWN until about 30 years ago, when it became an overspill town for Birmingham as part of the national New Town Development initiative. Redditch is also a manufacturing town, and many of the businesses and industries in the area are related to the car industry, because Rover, for example, is based about six miles away at Longbridge. The town's dependency on Rover is diminishing, however, because the company has consistently downsized and reorganised since it almost went into liquidation and was taken over by the German car giant BMW in the late 1990s.

Redditch has 33,750 households and a population of about 100,000. It is an area of contrast between affluence and poverty, and one that does not benefit from funding for neighbourhood renewal. Located in Worcestershire, Redditch does not immediately conjure up images of poverty; in fact, the Feckenham area of Redditch is in the top 10 per cent of most affluent wards in the country. Conversely, Batchley – a large housing estate – is in the top ten most disadvantaged wards nationally, although a new development of houses costing £100,000–£200,000 will make Batchley look good (or will at least take it out of the category of most deprived ward). This is good for Redditch as a whole, but it is not so good for the people who continue to live in poverty on the estate.

Redditch has pockets of deprivation, but they are hidden – because half the houses on some estates are owner occupied, while the other half are rented from the Council. This mixture hides poverty and distorts the ward's statistics. Redditch has a large number of single parents and is in the top 10 per cent of places with the most 'indebted individuals' in the West Midlands.

Redditch is a new town, so it has little history of political action and organisation. People in the town have become isolated, because town planners have carved up the town with round-abouts and dual carriageways that create borders and boundaries between the various sectors of the town. The new communities created in this process were meant to be self-contained and self-sustaining, but supermarkets offer free bus services to out-of-community areas and this has had a knock-on effect on local traders' ability to offer successful shopping services.

ALLEARN

ALLearn is a collaborative project that came out of the Redditch Lifelong Learning Network and was supported by funding from the Worcestershire Lifelong Learning Partnership. The partnership is chaired by Redditch Borough Council, which provides educational services to local residents on an area basis and focuses on the most-deprived communities. ALLearn is linked into, and works in partnership with, a number of agencies and area-based initiatives with respect to its planning and service provision. These include projects supported by the New Opportunities Fund, Sure Start and Inter Authorities Group.

I met with Michael Smith, manager of the Redditch Employment Development Initiative (REDI) centre, and Jenny Murray, regional project development manager of Interact 21, to find out how the ALLearn partnership was meeting the educational needs of the community. I wanted to know how local adult learning needs had been assessed, what type of provision had been put in place to meet these needs and what were partnership's plans for the future.

Assessment of learning needs

The ALLearn partnership carried out research to establish residents' views on adult and community learning in the various areas of the town. The main objective was to set up and test local management structures for learning in Redditch. The project initially focused on four geographical areas – Smallwood, Batchley, Woodrow and Church Hill; these were chosen because they had the highest levels of deprivation in the town and already had multi-agency alliances supported by Redditch Borough Council's Community Development Section in place. The project lasted from November 2000 to March 2001 and had three main tasks:

Reditch
ALLearn

- to collate baseline data on lifelong learning

- to set up a lifelong learning forum in each neighbourhood

- to create new learning opportunities.

Local people were trained to carry out the research and were supported by Interact 21. Questionnaires were distributed in the four key districts and a comprehensive household survey was performed in Church Hill. Residents were asked for information about the type of advice and guidance they had received in the past, who had supplied it and how useful it had been. They were asked if they had participated in, or were considering participating in, education and were asked to identify any barriers to participation.

The results of the survey in relation to barriers to participation were not surprising. Residents identified lack of childcare provision, previous bad experiences in education, stigma (of doing literacy courses, for example), transport problems, course costs and a poor range of course options as inhibitive factors.

The Bite Size Programme

This baseline assessment meant that partners in ALLearn were better placed to plan what services should be delivered, for whom and where, and how funding might be attracted to support future initiatives. The research's recommendations directly related to problems identified by local residents: costs of transport, lack of childcare, accessibility and lack of relevant courses. The research also recommended that learning opportunities should be provided in bite-sized, manageable chunks – this was essential for reluctant learners whose first-time experiences had not been favourable.

The detailed research on the Church Hill estate was crucial to the ALLearn partnership's success in securing £900,000 from the European Social Fund for a local learning centre. The centre will deliver adult learning opportunities from a refurbished community-based former school, starting from September 2002.

Embedding the initiative

Michael informed me that, 'Education and regeneration is important; at the end of the day, you need someone to spearhead initiatives rather than to pontificate." ALLearn cannot be accused of pontificating.

READY TO HELP OUT AT THE REDI RECEPTION DESK

The next step for the ALLearn Partnership was to take advantage of the 'Bite Size' programme, which enabled the partnership to put the research's recommendations into practice. Bite Size was an initiative supported by the Learning and Skills Council in 2001. Nationally, learning providers were given the opportunity to bid for financial support to run their own locally based education and training courses aimed at engaging adults in learning through – as the name suggests – a range of short courses. ALLearn won a bid for funding and ran a number of two-hour tasters for a variety of courses – from beauty to astrology and from Messy Play to fingernail painting. Michael explained that:

> Courses were made available from six to eight in the evening; all were based at the REDI Centre. Interact 21 also ran a number of Bite Size courses from their Internet café and some in the community. All Women's House also ran courses from their centre. The college ran some too. The initiatives were separate, but we made sure that courses did not overlap – our courses were phenomenally successful. We ran 11 tasters over a

four-week period in the evenings, and we had 110 people attend. We offered childcare to anyone who attended. These courses were run from March to June 2002.

Jenny further explained that:

We wanted to engage people who would not sign up to a longer course; we wanted to offer a taste of learning without learners having to make a commitment, to provide a series of short steps for those who wanted to take them, whilst making sure that no inhibiting factors were bearing on the learner's decision to get involved.

ALLearn wanted to the tasters to result in progression, but the partners were not sure could this be done – given the problem of getting people to sign up to long(ish) and perhaps accredited courses. Partners from the college (Widening Participation, All Women's House and REDI) discussed how they could encourage progression and continue to engage learners who had initially signed up to the Bite Size courses. They decided to continue their own version of Bite Size, but with slightly larger courses than included in the LSC-supported initiative. Courses lasting 3, 6 and 12 hours were offered in a range of curriculum areas; they were designed to excite and attract the curious and were all based in community settings. Michael explained that most of the programmes offered were designed to be accessed by people who wanted to progress. Different routes of progression are currently available, 'once they pass 12 hours, they are into accreditation in real terms – they can go for NVQ [National Vocational Qualification] or OCN [Open College Network] accreditation'. In terms of marketing, Jenny illustrated the importance of locally focused strategies:

We found that the flaw with Bite Size is that the national marketing campaign is known to be unsuccessful; we carried out lots of marketing – we marketed locally, leaflet-dropped and supported the whole initiative with outreach workers and community development teams.

ALLearn's Bite Size+ programme has three parts: the curriculum, learning advocates and confidence building, and childcare. Advocates are members of the community who are paid a nominal amount of money and are provided with training while still claiming benefits. The project's advocates will be employed from September 2002 to March 2003. If the project can be sustained after this time, ALLearn expects that it will naturally evolve to develop advocates into community tutors. Some of the learners and volunteers already associated with ALLearn's partner organisations will be well placed to become community advocates, because they are from the community and know the community's issues. The confidence-building aspect of Bite Size+ relates to the fact that advocates are working with people who have been failed by the education system. At each of the tasters, there will be an Inter Authorities Group. Bite Size+ will operate initially in the Woodrow area of Redditch.

Michael suggested that, if the Bite Size+ initiative can be developed after its first 'season', ALLearn may offer some courses from a central location in the future, but that 'at the moment, [we] believe that it will be more effective if we offer services to people on their own turf'. For this initiative to be effective for hard-to-reach groups, barriers to participation identified in the Church Hill household survey must be dismantled. Lack of adequate, and preferably free, childcare is a major barrier, and its provision is an essential part of the new initiative.

THE FUTURE FOR REDDITCH

I left the Redi Centre reflecting on the maps of the area that I'd seen and the way in which town planners had carved up Redditch with green, tree-lined dual carriageways, one-way systems and roundabouts. I had little sense of the town centre, because not a single resident was in sight. I couldn't help thinking that the ALLearn partnership was well on its way to developing learners and providing local people with skills and confidence in their own abilities. I considered that next time around town planners for Redditch would find it difficult to have a committee report on the future design of the town rubber stamped as a matter of course – the residents would be more likely to have their own views on neighbourhood renewal and planning developments in their town.

-5-

REACHING

OUT

INTO

COMMUNITIES

NORTHUMBERLAND COUNTY COUNCIL
Rural
In-reach

> The most effective approaches to community self-help have emerged in an organic way: community self-help is not something that can be imposed. Whereas some communities seem to have cracked the problem, with a wide variety of thriving community associations, others, without obvious distinguishing characteristics, are relatively unconnected, with limited community interaction. For these, skilled, professional intervention may be necessary.
>
> **POLICY ACTION TEAM 9 – COMMUNITY SELF-HELP**

Northumberland
County
Council

BEFORE RURAL IN-REACH, Northumberland had two schools – one high school and one middle school – with an adult education programme and a designated budget from the Learning and Skills Council. The budget was delegated through the Local Education Authority and enabled the schools to provide education services for adults. Both centres found it difficult to provide learning opportunities for people in rural areas, although some learners would come to the adult centres.

The area also had a project called Peritec, which was based around the provision of computers to village halls and was supported by the European Social Fund. When this initiative ended, the equipment was left redundant.

ESTABLISHING RURAL IN-REACH

Local learning providers intuitively knew that they were having a limited impact in rural communities. They needed to provide services for hard-to-reach villagers, who traditionally had very few educational services and were not too prone to taking advantage of what was available – for a variety of good reasons.

An informal partnership – the Rural In-reach partnership – was formed to find out what services people had taken advantage of in the past and to gain an insight into their needs. Funding was requested from the Adult and Community Learning Fund (ACLF) for a project to reach and engage hard-to-reach people in two upland areas of Northumberland – Upper Coquet and Wansbeck Valley. A bid for round two ACLF funding was developed and submitted, but it was unsuccessful because there had not been enough community involvement when it was put together. A subsequent bid for round three funding, which was half the size of the original bid and was compiled in partnership with the two community schools – Rothbury Computer

Association and the Northumberland Open College Network, was successful.

Rural In-reach aimed to provide accessible learning opportunities and to investigate and devise strategies to encourage people into mainstream learning. The project also intended to contribute to the Northumberland Lifelong Learning Plan, with a particular focus on raising awareness of rural needs, problems and priorities and encouraging statutory providers to tackle the problems and find ways to make rural provision sustainable.

The County Council became accountable for Rural In-reach, because the informal partnership had no legal identity in its own right. The County Council contributed to an overall steering group that was responsible for the day-to-day running of the project and management decisions. Caroline (Carrie) Tulett, who was local to the area and knew something of the local issues, was recruited as the development manager. She was given a small budget, part-time administrative support and six weeks to decide what to do in the following two and a half years.

I met with Carrie to discuss the project and the problems in Upper Coquet and Wansbeck Valley. She explained that the population density of the area is similar to some of the less populated areas of Sweden, with about 10,000 people living in a very large rural community. Most activities in the Upper Coquet and Wansbeck valley revolve around farming – principally upland sheep farming. Some forestry and quarrying work exists, and a local reservoir has a small, tight-knit community based around the water-treatment works. The local authority is the

GETTING TO GRIPS WITH LEARNING

biggest employer in Northumberland, and the whole county has about 20 large employers and leans towards small and medium enterprises.

The area also has a strong landed gentry and estates culture, with a number of tied properties and rented accommodation. In some places, the cultural differences in terms of wealth and property type are quite stark. Some of the wards fall into the deprivation indices, but quite a few do not have many residents, so the statistics can be deceptive. The communities have established meeting patterns and places that provide good community focal points from which services could be delivered.

Participation rates are very localised. For example, the participation rates in Rothbury, which has a school, library and so on, are fair – about 10 per cent; one mile outside the village, however, participation rates are only about 3 per cent. One of the many issues to emerge from Carrie's research, 'Rural learning, An investigation into the barriers and solutions to widening participation in rural areas', was that people generally are not prepared to travel for courses and educational opportunities. According to Carrie's research:

> **It is estimated that rural people make up approximately 34 per cent of the functionally illiterate, [this is] surprising given the focus on literacy needs of the inner-city. With the collapse of most natural resource-based economies, literacy poses a formidable barrier to the rural people who now seek employment in more sophisticated markets. Adult literacy programmes in rural areas are quite fragile and to make them more effective we need to involve salaried staff and energise development work.**

Carrie quickly identified that the Rural In-reach partnership needed a distinct identity with which local people could connect. The partnership also required some legal identity to support its continued development and strategy, so a registered charity, with its own board of trustees, was formed. The Rural In-reach project was delivered effectively by the charity, which became known as 'Learning Choices', on a contracted basis. The project included five initiatives:

- Learning Parishes
- Learning Bank
- Learning IT
- Learning Communities
- Learning Circles

Learning Parishes

Learning Parishes was the first initiative introduced. As the first phase of the project, it used detailed research to identify barriers to, and solutions to increase, participation in learning in rural communities. This first initiative devised methods by which the other four could market-test solutions and contribute to an overall project evaluation. In effect, Carrie and her colleagues tried out and monitored a range of services to see what worked and what did not work. This research prompted recommendations for future action.

Learning Bank

The Learning Bank was one of the first resource and educational facilities to be established with the ACLF's funding and was Rural In-Reach's second initiative. The Learning Bank was held in a central point, and a catalogue listed the available items, which included laptops, fundraising guides, art materials and digital cameras. Community groups, individuals and tutors could use the resources free of charge to stimulate learning activities for various education and learning purposes. Carrie explained:

> **People could simply take the equipment away on loan or there was training offered with these resources when people or groups required it. One person wanted to produce a**

newsletter, and we guided them through the process. Other people were doing self-programming and family learning-type activities. Local people ran these initiatives themselves in village halls and central community locations. There were 13 village halls in the area that we dealt with and we used every one of them for events, course, exhibitions and the like.

The Learning Bank was a logical early step, because the funding money had to be spent in a short period of time, because materials and equipment in rural communities were limited and outdated, and because outdated computer 'kit' was available from past initiatives, such as Peritec.

Learning IT

The third initiative was 'Learning IT', which involved training the trainers to be better equipped to manage and organise information technology (IT) provision.

Although Learning IT provides IT and basic skills training, it also has been the hub of a centrally coordinated bid for six community associations to develop IT centres and to re-energise the efforts of the Peritec programme. The Learning IT initiative aims to provide centres of excellence in graphics and digital art, music technology, IT for farmers and consistently high-standard core services, such as access to the Internet, email and software. The project intends to seek support from charitable trusts, The Countryside Agency, Europe and other key sources
.

Learning Communities

Community groups were mostly informal, employed few people and had limited infrastructures. Carrie and her team helped groups with training and development and to put together development plans, constitutions and, in some cases, applications for financial support. Some training was basic and short term – for example, providing guidance on how to become a registered charity; other training extended over a much longer period and effected greater changes – training on fundraising, for example.

At the request of local people, communities were offered a wide range of vocational and non-vocational training. Specialist tutors were brought in to teach the subjects people asked for. Carrie informed me that:

One of the unique projects that we did was to offer four weeks of tasters in pubs, clubs, village halls, etc. In September, full programmes were going to be run from the two community schools, so we better prepared people for these courses by giving them the chance to 'try before you buy', talk to tutors and other potential learners and help them to make much more informed choices about the suitability of the courses. Sixty per cent of those who came onto the taster course went onto do other courses, 35 per cent went to the community schools and 25 per cent to the learning communities project. The function of this exercise was to provide progression routes, though this is not a main aim of the initiative, but [is] an important one.

Learning Circles

This phase of development matched providers with potential learners through a variety of tried and tested and innovative marketing techniques. Local networks were used extensively to promote learning opportunities: parish and community newsletters, the free press, local television stations and websites were a few of the tried and tested methods used. Direct faxes and emails sent to potential learners and the use of local people to promote opportunities were particularly successful.

NEIGHBOURHOOD RENEWAL

The work carried out as part of the Rural In-reach project has had significant implications for neighbourhood renewal. It has supported the establishment of groups that have not previously existed, enabled existing community groups to be able to make their own decisions, nurtured an awareness of developments outside village communities that significantly impact upon them and enabled learners to plan in the long term and create a vision of where they are going. A prime example of this is the creative, collaborative and strategic action taken by the people who live in the village of Mitford.

Mitford

Mitford village had always had a post office that was in one of the villager's houses. The owners sold the house, but the new owners did not want to take over the post office service. The loss of the post office would have left the village pub as the only place for community focus, and villagers realised that this would have been a vital blow to the village and its ability to sustain itself for any length of time. The Rural In-reach programme had been running training sessions on funding with the village hall committee. A planning session explored villagers' hopes and dreams for the village hall and discussed the need to have a vision when applying for financial support – rather than simply applying for funding because it is available. As part of the session, everyone was asked to write down their thoughts and ideas about the community centre on flipcharts. Practically everyone wanted a shop and a post office.

Many people in the village were of retirement age, but this did not hinder their pursuit of a vision for a new shop and

LEARNING TO PARTICIPATE

Northumberland
County
Council

78

post office. Rural In-reach provided community business training and advice on how to negotiate with the Parish Council, The Countryside Agency and the Post Office:

We got the villagers to get in touch with the Post Office and negotiate what they wanted, and lo and behold, they came out and did some examinations of the hall to make sure that it was suitable, and eventually the post office was put into the village hall (the extension). It was opened a few months ago, and villagers are now looking for funding to rebuild their village hall; hoping to be able to open and provide a community shop – their shop – they have sought and got planning permission to build a new hall to accommodate it.

Rural ecosystems

Rural ecosystems can be very fragile because they are tied into environmental forces, such as the weather, the growing and harvesting seasons, and the lifecycles, parasites and diseases of animals. The 2001 outbreak of foot and mouth disease had a great impact on rural communities in Northumberland and on the Rural In-Reach's work with villagers. People literally stayed in their homes, and the outbreak had psychological effects for everyone, as people had to be disinfected as they went into and left communities. The outbreak was a time of great uncertainty that lasted about 11 months.

The Rural In-reach team responded by providing telephone support, sending out information and resource packs, arranging email conferences and utilising Learndirect. When people were able to return to the village halls, they were given the chance to make up for lost time. About 90 per cent of people came back, and those who did not were still subject to restrictions. The restrictions ended in about February 2002 and, at this time, learning activities were taken back into the communities.

RURAL RESEARCH STUDY

The presentation of the findings from the rural research study was the final phase of the project and provided a basis for further action and evidence to illustrate the needs of learners in rural communities. One of the main barriers to learning for residents in rural areas is the time it takes to travel: people will not travel more than seven miles for learning, although those already engaged in learning will travel 10 miles.

Carrie's research was carried out through direct consultation in two valleys in north Northumberland. It aimed to discover the best methods to deliver learning activities to reach local people. Learning patterns and barriers were fully assessed through an 18-month programme of investigation, pilots and evaluation.

The research showed that rural areas are so diverse that it can be difficult to approach issues from a nationwide perspective. Planners often have little understanding of the unique circumstances in rural communities. As a result, those who work at grassroots level are often frustrated that their challenges are not understood.

The final analysis of the research explains that:

The volume driven finance policies are limiting curriculum and programme development, and centres are finding it increasingly difficult to harness learners…for those in education, enrolment-driven finance formulas make it increasingly difficult to respond to dispersed populations. Centralisation also seems to contribute towards a loss of diversity, especially with regard to the curriculum.

The rural research study already is available on CD, but it is hoped to publish it as a book, so that its results can be shared as widely as possible. The research model and findings have been given to the Learning and Skills Development Agency, Department for Education and Skills, National Institute of Adult Continuing Education, Learning and Skills Council and the Local Education Authority (LEA).

The LEA has used the model, and fundraising efforts headed up by Carrie have led to the release of over £500,000 to energise rural development work. This project, called Awakening Learning, started in June 2002 and will run until December 2003. Rural In-Reach hopes that the project will become self-sustaining, as word of mouth and strong development work attracts large numbers of people.

The study and Rural In-reach pilot have also enabled Learning Choices to tap into funds in the following areas: money for rural learning, Information, Advice and Guidance Partnership roadshows, Learn Direct roadshows, a rural basic skills and IT project, and Doing IT on the Farm. A recent project in community arts is likely to be extended, so that renewal of community activities profoundly affected by the foot and mouth outbreak can be continued.

THE FUTURE OF LEARNING CHOICES

Learning Choices' current work involves developing new methods to attract rural learners. Rather than becoming a mainstream provider, it has continued to be an active demonstration project that shows people possible ways forward for rural learning. In addition to the demonstration work, Learning Choices also continues to develop informal community-led learning opportunities that cannot be supported by mainstream funding but that may be an important first step for community regeneration and renewal. The effective coordination and working of partners, coupled with Carrie's research recommendations and insights, will provide the skills and knowledge and the excitement and expertise to enliven villagers in their learning.

Northumberland County Council

81

GRANTHAM COLLEGE – YES4LEARNING
Taking learning out into the community with the Sat Van

‘For people living in low-income neighbourhoods, gaining and exploiting ICT [Information and Communications Technology] skills can lead to opportunities to participate fully in the local and national economy. The arguments for social inclusion and for economic development in the Information age ate mutually reinforcing.’

POLICY ACTION TEAM 15 – INFORMATION TECHNOLOGY

GRANTHAM IN LINCOLNSHIRE IS A QUIET and unassuming, small rural town that centres on the high street that forms the main shopping area. The people of Grantham work in a range of service industries, mainly associated with food processing, packing and preparation, but there is some industrial development, with small business units in a number of industrial estates. Grantham is described as a 'very working-class town' and has at least two disadvantaged housing estates in Earlsfield and Harrowby.

The Yes4Learning initiative, based at Grantham College, provides a range of new services for the people of Grantham. The initiative has invested significantly in e-learning by developing an impressive e-learning suite within the college; it also has a special focus on 'distributed learning' within rural and generally hard-to-reach communities.

Yes4Learning has operated from the Stonebridge Road wing of Grantham College and a number of support bases within various local communities since September 2001. The initiative is receiving support for a three-year period from the New Opportunities Fund, and it is an example of partnership working, innovation and creative outreach. I met Catherine Johnson, ICT (Information and Communications Technology) facilitator, and Tom Crowther, ICT technician, to find out more about Yes4 Learning and the Satellite Van.

MAIN AIMS OF YES4LEARNING

Yes4Learning is aimed primarily at individuals who missed out on traditional education in the past, local businesses and people who live in isolated rural communities. Courses on offer range from general interest and information technology skills through to personal and professional development programmes. Programmes also are available for those seeking to improve their numeracy, literacy and spoken English. Courses are available in the Earlesfield and New Beacon areas of the town and at the George Centre on Grantham High Street. A partner of Yes4Learning – Yes4Business – will visit the premises of local companies. The Yes4Learning website (www.yes4learning.org.uk/) informs the reader that:

There are a number of values that underpin everything at yes. These include accessibility; flexibility; responsiveness; friendliness and inclusiveness. The learners that yes will target are currently excluded from education for a wide range of reasons including social, economic, age, location, time and cost – yes will work hard to remove these barriers as far as possible. The curriculum offered will be tailored to meet individual needs around a core of Information Technology and Basic Skills provision. A mix of recreational and vocational courses will also be offered in addition to meet demand.

THE SATELLITE VAN

The Satellite Van, or Sat Van, is one of Yes4Learning's strategies for working with and engaging people from hard-to-reach groups. In the case of some of Grantham's more remote areas, this mean groups that literally are hard to reach because of their geographical location or because they have problems getting to the e-learning base at the main college.

I was shown the Sat Van – a state-of-the-art piece of technical wizardry that is able to access the Internet through a remotely controlled, rotating satellite dish on top of the van. The main aim of the van is to take technology to hard-to-reach communities. The van contains relatively standard computer hardware – a monitor, keyboard, hard drive and mouse – but it also has a generator to power its own electricity supply, a server to support internet access and, of course, the motor-driven satellite dish, as well as a complex mass of wires, plugs and boards. Yes4Learning have owned the van, which has a striking presence, for about six months. The van is a prototype and one of only a handful in the country – Boston College has a similar van, as – apparently – does Edinburgh University.

The Sat Van travels to a venue – for example, a village hall where it is to deliver a taster course to a group of older learners – and sets up for the session. So that the van's satellite dish and the

IT LEARNING IN GRANTHAM COLLEGE

extraterrestrial satellite (Telstar 12) can exchange uninterrupted signals, the van parks at least two metres away from solid objects, such as walls or trees, and with a specific angle between the satellite and dish (which does not rotate in a complete circle). The tutor activates the satellite dish and then sets up as many laptop computers as required – usually about 12 – in the venue. Each laptop contains a remotely controlled network card that is fitted with two tiny antennae that enable communication between the satellite dish and the laptop.

Meanwhile, a technician in the Sat Van sets up a wire-less network. The satellite talks to the van's modem through the satellite dish, the modem talks to the server and the server sends a signal through Sat Van's antenna to the laptops in the village hall. Simple!

AREA-BASED LEARNING

Catherine explained that learners take advantage of a variety of services and courses through the Sat Van. These can range from six-hour taster courses to the 60-hour Computer Literacy and Information Technology (CLAIT) course. Some learners use courses for very specific functions, such as establishing e-mail contact with friends and family members in different parts of the world and improving their employability.

TOM CROWTHER, IT TECHNICIAN, GRANTHAM COLLEGE

Yes4Learning provides a range of area-based services to support the van, including Yes@George (in the town centre), Yes@Harrowby (an out-of-town housing estate), Yes@Earlsfield (another housing estate) and Yes@Thecollege. All of these support services offer a range of options that are client centred and flexible in terms of their level of accreditation (if accreditation is appropriate), their duration and their method of delivery. Yes4Learning also provides 'value-added' services, such as crèche facilities, which are offered free of charge or at a reduced rate for the unwaged and those on low incomes, and the Sat Van, which already has had a significant impact on the college's ability to reach people in remote parts of Grantham.

WORKING WITH BUSINESS

Yes4Business is Yes4Learning's partner project and business arm. The main service Yes4Business offers is bespoke training for companies – either at their offices or at the town-based premises in the George Centre. Before any training begins, Yes4Business undertakes a needs analysis so the training can be tailored to the company's specific needs. Where possible, training leads to a national qualification.

Yes4Business also delivers on-the-job training; this provides real links to neighbourhood renewal, in that it gives employed people training and learning opportunities that they would not have otherwise. For a shift worker completing a shift at 10.00 pm, learning services can be provided on-the-job after the shift.

Ultimately, Yes4Learning and Yes4Business are about responding to learners' needs and about changing people's perception of education and learning. The team at Yes:

have high hopes that yes will begin to break down barriers to learning in new and innovative ways and will enable individuals to expand their horizons, develop skills for life and realise their personal ambitions.

Courses are open to everyone, regardless of age or previous qualifications, with advice and guidance available to inform individuals of the best programme for their particular need.

Grantham
College –
Yes4Learning

-6-

NEIGHBOURHOOD

RENEWAL IN

RESIDENTIAL

AREAS

LONDON AND QUADRANT HOUSING
Residents
online

> People who live in deprived neighbourhoods are less likely to be able to use the most common methods of training or points of access to ICT [Information and Communications Technologies]. This presents particular problems. Many people in deprived neighbourhoods are unemployed, and as a result, do not get hands-on supported ICT experience that many do through their work. They also have often had off-putting educational experiences in the past, and tend to find formal training unattractive.
>
> POLICY ACTION TEAM 15 – INFORMATION TECHNOLOGY

LONDON AND QUADRANT HOUSING TRUST

THE LONDON AND QUADRANT HOUSING TRUST works in partnership with many local authorities across London in regeneration and neighbourhood renewal projects. Each project is approached in a holistic way, and consultation with local people allows the Trust to offer a tailored solution for each area in which they work. The physical rebuilding or refurbishment of homes is part of their core business, but the Trust acknowledges that it needs to encourage a raft of other initiatives to ensure the future of vibrant, sustainable communities. Some of the Trust's largest regeneration projects are in Edmonton (Green Horizons), Silwood Estate, Leyton (Forest Homes) and Feltham in West London.

Quadrant Community Investment (QCI) – the Trust's development arm – specialises in the Trust's 'people' work and provides funding to empower people to make their neighbourhoods popular places to live. The Trust has become an acknowledged expert organisation in the use of ICT in regeneration. Residents Online, the Silwood Cybercentre and the UK Online centre in the Trust's foyer in Crawley are flagship projects under the QCI umbrella.

The London and Quadrant Housing Trust owns 30,000 homes across London and the South East. The Trust's residents all live in rented housing. One-third of residents are single parent families, less than one-quarter work full-time, 45 per cent are unemployed or not seeking work, 8 per cent are disabled and just over 36 per cent are from ethnic minorities. Many of the Trust's residents have no formal qualifications, low levels of self-confidence and a sense of lack of progress in their lives. In short, many could be thought of as socially excluded.

The Trust firmly believes that housing associations are ideally placed to reach those who are socially excluded and to help them gain the skills and access to ICT that will help them benefit from the information age. The Trust also sees a relation between acquiring and using new ICT skills and neighbourhood renewal and community engagement. This is reflected in the mobile courses offered to residents, which typically seek to empower local people.

RESIDENTS ONLINE

Residents Online is a partnership project between London and Quadrant Housing Trust and its residents. The project comprises a mobile ICT learning programme and a website (www.residentsonline.org.uk). The Residents Online project was kick-started by an Innovation and Good Practice Grant awarded by the Housing Corporation when the Trust won the National Housing Federation's Best Communications in Housing Award in December 1998. This grant paid for the building of the website and a pilot learning programme.

The running of the project was funded by the Adult and Community Learning Fund (ACLF) until June 2001. Since then, funding has been provided by the New Opportunities Fund and the Department for Education and Skills as part of the UK Online initiative. The Trust also financially supports the programme through Quadrant Community Investment – a fund that is strongly linked with the Trust's neighbourhood renewal work.

One of the major aims of Residents Online was to tackle technological exclusion by encouraging residents, whenever possible, to surf the web, use e-mail and generally get online. This aim involved running a series of mobile training sessions for interested residents, placing more than 100 web-ready computers in resident groups and giving free internet access through a London cyber café.

The ICT courses, which are delivered on a suite of laptops that are moved from place to place, help residents learn new skills. As residents' become more confident, they may begin to put across information and opinions within public arenas. The Trust also strives to recognise new talent through its Business Development Fund, which is administered through QCI.

Since 1999, the Residents Online project has achieved everything its steering panel set out to do – and more. The three strands of the project are all moving forward in line with its original targets:

The learning programme is a huge hit with residents. A total of 348 residents have been trained since the project started, and over 400 residents are on the waiting list. Five residents regularly help as mentors. The free learning programmes, which involve at least 12 hours of teaching, are the most popular 'offer' Residents Online has ever made through its residents magazine, Homelife.

The website is at the heart of the project and is kept up to date by the Trust's staff and residents. The bulletin board, accessed from the website's home page, is evidence of the ongoing support and enthusiasm of residents. The online repairs service was developed at the suggestion of residents and is a key interactive feature of the site. It was the first online repairs service in the United Kingdom.

Internet-ready computers have been given to most of the Trust's residents' associations through recycled machines supplied by Computers for Charity. One session of every learning programme is held in a public cyber café to ensure that residents are at ease using them. A list of cyber cafés is featured on the website.

The project has been driven from the start by a panel of committed residents who make decisions on the content of the website and the shape and direction of the learning programme. Lewisham College is a partner in the project with the Trust.

At present, the Trust takes the courses to wherever there is demand – even if this means dashing halfway across London with a taxi full of laptops for an impromptu training session for a residents' association. A suite of eight laptops is taken from place to place on a regular basis.

Gareth Schweitzer, the Residents Online tutor, has run 57 courses in 23 different locations since January 2000. The programme's popularity is due in part to the amount of telephone contact Gareth has with future learners, reassuring and advising them.

The Trust also ensures that the place, pace and atmosphere of the sessions is fun, informal and stress-free. Every resident who completes a course receives a certificate that outlines the content they have covered. Learners are encouraged to continue learning, and Lewisham College offers an e-guidance service via e-mail, through which learners can get advice on available courses and career moves.

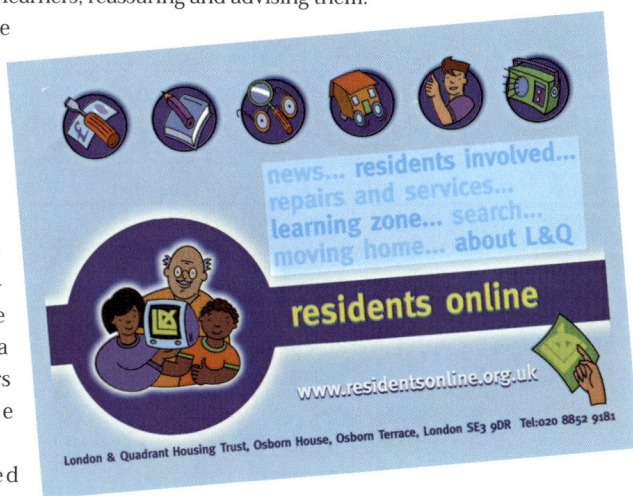

news... residents involved... repairs and services... learning zone... search... moving home... about L&Q

residents online

www.residentsonline.org.uk

London & Quadrant Housing Trust, Osborn House, Osborn Terrace, London SE3 9DR Tel:020 8852 9181

Residents in sheltered schemes have been some of the project's most enthusiastic learners. A free computer has been placed in the common room in six of the sheltered schemes that have benefited from learning schemes. These facilities are well used, and demand grows for more courses among the Trusts 'Silver Surfer' population.

Recent additions to the project have been website design courses for people with computer skills and a computer "warm-up" course for absolute beginners. Residents who attend the website design course can build a website for their residents' association, community group or even their own small business. Five websites built by residents are linked to the Residents Online site.

COMPUTERS, RESIDENTS, LEARNING AND NEIGHBOURHOOD RENEWAL

Computers are often seen as the twenty-first century's solution to a wide range of problems. They enable the young and old alike to become better learners and provide an impetus for the development of business through better marketing, management and accounting. Computers need individuals to operate them, however, and those individuals have to see the value and benefit of using them. The project's work is essential in helping residents to alleviate any fears they have about new technologies and to explore various ways in which computers can make a difference in, and be an important aid to, their lives.

Residents are most likely to see the value of computers if they see that computers can help them get where they want to be or can help them perform specific tasks of importance. After all, the acquisition of computer skills is not an end in itself – it's important to be able to apply newly acquired skills. Many residents also hope that their newly acquired ICT skills will provide a route to employment and an escape from the 'benefits trap'.

When the Trust talks about regeneration, it is talking about its mission to create places where people want to live. It acknowledges that this does not only relate to improving the physical environment but is also about empowering people and providing new opportunities. One of the most powerful opportunities the Trust can give people is access to computers and learning programmes that take people where they want to go. The use of computers and 'high

London and Quadrant Housing

technology' can provide plenty of opportunities – whether getting in contacting family or friends, looking for a job on the Internet or doing an accredited training course through a UK Online centre

Chloe Douglas: a stunning ambassador

Chloe Douglas, a resident of the Trust who attended a five-week Residents Online Learning Programme in February 2000, is an excellent ambassador for the project. Chloe was enthusiastic and quick to pick up new skills. As the training progressed, she became a key member of the group and readily helped others who were finding it difficult to master the skills.

At the time of the learning programme, Chloe was going through a difficult time at home; now she says that the Residents Online course came along just at the right time. It gave her a new interest and prevented her getting too downcast about her problems. After completing the course, Chloe was asked to become a member of the residents' panel that drives the Residents Online Programme. She agreed and has been an invaluable member of the group, with a wealth of ideas on how to develop the project.

Chloe has now joined the project as a mentor, and she regularly helps the learning programmes. She has proved to be a very able communicator and a patient helper. Recently, she was asked to help Maggie Gebbett, communications manager, produce a presentation about the project to a high-profile audience of 500 people. She took up the challenge and overcome any nervousness, proving herself as an able speaker and, as Maggie put it, 'a stunning ambassador for the project'.

Chloe attended a conference arranged by the Tenant Participation Advisory Service last year and helped present the Residents Online Project to other tenants. She has also helped with some of the administration of the project by seeking out new learning venues and providing telephone support to encourage new tenants to attend courses.

Chloe, like many other women who have benefited from Resident Online training courses, relishes the opportunity of having time to be herself, rather than being somebody's mum (as honourable as that is). Chloe recently started work for the Trust as administrator at the newly opened UK Online centre at Silwood Estate, Lewisham.

Silwood Cybercentre

The Trust is always keen to follow up new opportunities to use ICT in its regeneration and neighbourhood renewal work. Where possible, the Trust opens new centres and provides employment to help meet the needs of residents and build community capacity.

Silwood Estate on the borders of Lewisham and Southwark is home to one of London's best cybercentres – one that recently won the national award for best UK Online centre in London. The centre, which can accommodate up to 25 learners at a time, offers a variety of free learning programmes and the drop-in use of computers with fast Internet access. People who want to become computer support workers can attend a groundbreaking PC Technician's course.

One of the first people to come on the PC Technician's course at Silwood was Gulsen Huseyin. A local Silwood resident, she said:

> When I heard the centre was opening, I couldn't believe my luck. I am now well into my 12-week free course to become a PC Support Worker, and I am also brushing up on my computer skills. Some days, I'll help people who are completely new to computers. For many, it's a brand new experience to use a mouse. The centre has added a new dimension in my life. I want to increase my skills and get a job that uses them.

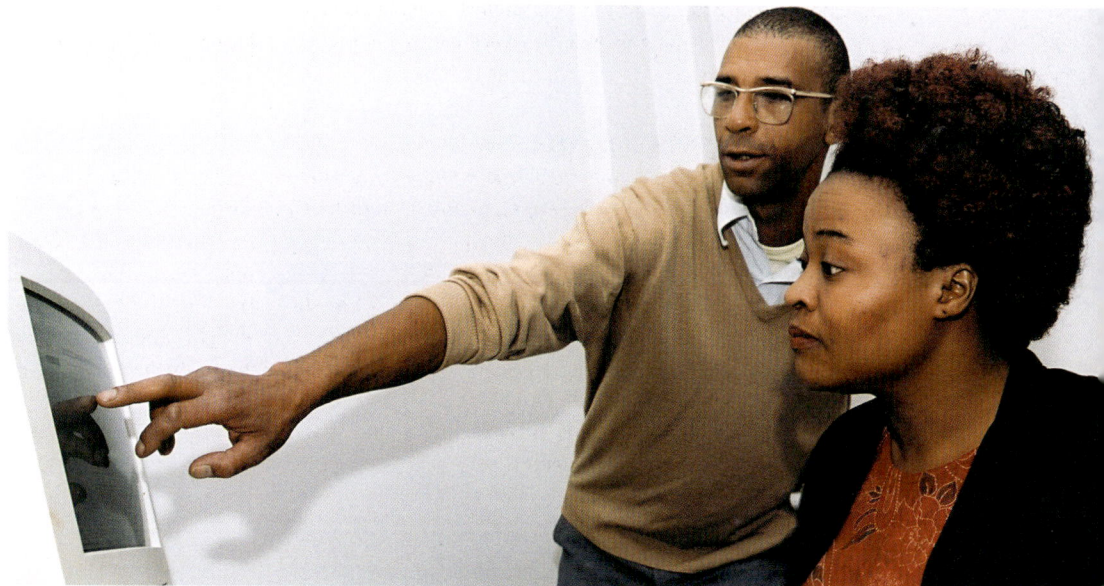

TREVOR CATTERICK, RESIDENTS ONLINE MENTOR, GIVES SOME HANDY TIPS

More information about Silwood Cybercentre can be found by visiting its website (www.silwoodonline.org.uk).

Trevor Catterick – the role of the mentor

The role of mentor is never far from the thoughts, planning and strategies that the Trust applies to its various projects. It is not unusual for a project participant to come back to the Trust in a variety of guises, for further training or for employment – as in the case of Chloe. Another such example is Trevor Catterick.

Trevor has worked on the Trust's Residents Online project since its inception in 1999 and attended one of the first courses. His involvement includes being a member of the steering group that oversees the work of the project, an employed mentor on the learning programme and an IT support worker on the project. Trevor comes across as a very quiet and serious man, but there is more to him than meets the eye. As project leader Maggie Gebbett explained:

> **Once you know Trevor better, you realise that he has clear ideas about how things should be run and will express his views with feeling. His observations are often penetrating and perceptive.**

Trevor now has a sound knowledge of using the Internet and e-mail and has helped at more than 15 of the Trust's learning programmes. Trevor has assisted in the set up of the suite of laptops taken to flexible learning programmes, ensuring that the Internet connection is made and supporting the delivery of the learning programme. He covers use of the Internet, search engines, basic HTML and using e-mails with attachments.

Trevor helps to keep a range of computers of various ages in working order. He also sets up machines in sheltered schemes and 'troubleshoots' when things go wrong. Trevor also sets up internet service providers (ISPs) for the Trust's community computers and ensures they are smooth running and glitch-free.

Staff members at the Trust have seen Trevor's confidence grow since he started working with them, and they are confident in his ability. He relates well to people in one-to-one situations and is a tremendous support worker. His knowledge and sound understanding of how to keep computers and networks working has added to his self-confidence, and this makes him an invaluable mentor. Staff on the project were delighted when Trevor found a full-time job after 15 years of unemployment. The Trust believes that this sort of case study shows the long-term benefits of this approach to community regeneration.

Not having had a job for a number of years, Trevor no doubt approaches new challenges and his full-time job with some trepidation, but he has the full backing and confidence of staff as he continues to grow as an invaluable team member.

Maria Jagger: from administration to project management

Maria Jagger, already an active member in her community, came on a Residents Online course in website design. After the three-day course, she produced a website for her residents' group (www.actionchattenden.org.uk). At the time, Maria was working as an administration officer on general maintenance contracts at Kingsnorth Power Station. Maria said:

The Residents Online course in 2000 gave me real confidence to go ahead and try new things. I had computer skills but had not used anything like a web design package before. It gave me a sense of being able to tackle new projects. I've now tried a number of PC applications and have the confidence just to work my way through them, even though I have no formal qualifications in ICT.

MARIA JAGGER TOOK A THREE-DAY WEB DESIGN COURSE AND NOW COORDINATES 15 UK ONLINE CENTRES.

Last year, Maria applied for and was offered a job as project manager for Medway Council. She is now in charge of getting 15 UK Online centres up and running in the area. She helps run Bite Size courses and does other teaching. Maria's current project is to set up a website that brings all the Medway Online centres together in one web portal.

MAKING A DIFFERENCE

The London and Quadrant Housing Trust is an award-winning company in the housing sector. Apart from holding the Chartermark, which recognises excellent customer service, the Trust has won a number of national awards for Residents Online and a prestigious national education award (Becta) for the Residents Online website. Judges of the Becta/The Guardian UK School and College Web Site Awards 2002 said that Residents Online was 'easy-to-use and engaging', and the site won the 'Community Education Whole-Site' category. The site has news and advice for residents, a kids 'n' teens club with competitions, and a talent showcase. Residents can ask questions and report their repair needs online. Chief Executive of Becta, Owen Lynch, said:

> **Community websites can play a role in encouraging learners of all ages to become involved. I am proud of the extensive range of educational content now available online. These resources, when properly used, can enrich the experience of anyone who wants to learn.**

The Trust is championing the use of ICT in the community. It believes that housing providers are in an excellent position to reach people who are socially excluded, disillusioned with traditional education provision and often caught in the 'benefits trap'.

Maggie Gebbett, project leader of Residents Online, says:

> **We are on a mission here to use ICT as a vehicle to reach people, build their skills and confidence, increase community capacity and ultimately make a difference in neighbourhood renewal. Our ICT work is just one strand of the mix that we try and tailor to every neighbourhood in which we work. We have seen some really exciting success stories through Residents Online and our other ICT work. But there are challenges too. The funding of these projects tends to be short term, and there is a lot of bureaucracy to master. But the government has shown its commitment to online Britain and has put in money to a number of initiatives to help everyone get up to speed with the information age. What is important is to get everyone aware of the technology of the Internet and e-mail, even if they are not experts in using them. We believe that in the same way that almost every home has a fridge and a video now, in future every home will have at least one computer. Socially excluded people don't want to be technologically excluded too, and ICT can be a powerful and popular route to reach people in neighbourhood renewal.**

London and
Quadrant
Housing

For further information, email Maggie Gebbett, communications manager, London and Quadrant Housing on mgebbett@lqgroup.org.uk or visit the Trust's website (www.lqgroup.org.uk).

BRAUNSTONE ESTATE IN LEICESTER
Braunstone
Motor Project

> 'Its distance from the city centre isolates Braunstone, an outer city estate.
> A swathe of outer city council estates runs from the north of Leicester to
> the south, Braunstone being the south westernmost. To the north and east,
> a railway separates the estate from a small industrial estate and an area
> of largely private semi-detached and terraced houses.'
>
> BRAUNSTONE NEW DEAL FOR COMMUNITIES BID, 2000

LOCAL SOLUTIONS TACKLE BIG PROBLEMS

THE DESCRIPTION OF BRAUNSTONE ESTATE, above, was given in the New Deal for Braunstone Delivery Plan. Braunstone Hall lies in the centre of the estate and is situated within the local park, which – together with the local parish church of St Peters and a few remaining cottages – is all that remains of the old country estate that was Braunstone. Leicester City Council purchased Braunstone in the 1920s, and in the 1930s built one of the largest public sector housing estates in the country. The estate was built for artisans, but it later provided cheap housing as city slum areas were cleared.

Today, Braunstone is described as a 'deprived community' that is struggling to meet the challenges of social and economic deprivation. The key deprivation indicators are that Braunstone has the highest mortality rates in Leicester, poor housing, the second highest level of unemployment in the city, a high crime rate and low rates of pay –the average household has an income of £8,480.

Appearances can be deceptive. I visited Braunstone on a sunny afternoon in early July and saw a quiet and well-organised estate, that comprises 5,050 households and almost 13,000 residents. I drove to my destination – the Braunstone Motor Project – and could not help but notice that each house was highly individual, with residents paying great attention to detail in the way they presented their houses. This meant that although almost all houses were identical in construction, they all looked different. It also meant that Braunstone residents were like residents anywhere else in the country in their aspirations, but that their aspirations remain largely unfulfilled because of a range of social and economic factors – including high levels of social deprivation and unemployment. Behind the 5,050 doors are a range of stories and a range of experiences.

There is light at the end of the tunnel for Braunstone, however, as demonstrated through a wide variety of initiatives and the benefit of New Deal for Community status. The residents of Braunstone are optimistic about the potential these initiatives have to change their lives and life chances for the better. There is also innovation in Braunstone and a real sense that local people are exploring local solutions to tackle problems such as poor housing and health care. This is illustrated in the fact that Braunstone New Deal for Communities is one of only two in the country that is community led: it has 12 local residents on its board, a range of other partners from housing, health and the private sector, and one member of Leicester City Council. I came to Braunstone to sample local innovation and the role of adult and community learning in neighbourhood renewal – I readily found this in the Braunstone Motor Project.

BRAUNSTONE MOTOR PROJECT

The Braunstone Motor Project is a registered charity that has been running for nine years and offers a range of off- and on-road activities. The Project aims to work with as many people as possible – initially within the Braunstone area, but then through the rest of the city and county. The Project aims to provide a facility that helps reduce the effects of poverty and enhance the quality of life for people within the inner city area by introducing activities not usually available to them and highlighting the positive results of such activities.

The project achieves its aims by teaching coordination and concentration skills, increasing the confidence of those that lack it and providing a range of opportunities that would not usually be available. All initiatives are about 'education through enjoyment', explained project administrator, Wayne Naylor.

The project was originally set up as a training and recreational facility with multi-agency involvement. The original idea was conceived through the North Braunstone Area Review Forum and its local Police and Community Subgroup, which expressed a need for a project to address local environmental and social issues by providing training, guidance and opportunities for young people, the unemployed and those with a tendency to commit car crime.

Braunstone Estate in Leicester

I met with Wayne, who coordinates a range of projects from the Project's base in the centre of the estate. The administration centre for the Project is a prime example of how locally based regeneration initiatives should be 'joined up'. The first part of the building is a shop front with a reception area and a number of young adults employed to help residents search for jobs and activities and complete application forms for jobs. Towards the back of the building, several young adults were working with a tutor to improve their basic skills and pursue their own areas of interest, such as graphic design.

MANY OF THE HOUSES ON BRAUNSTONE ESTATE ARE BOARDED UP

At the very far end of the building is a crèche for children of residents who wish to take advantage of the Project's many initiatives, which range from gardening to engineering. The local college supports the crèche, and youngsters are able to work towards various nursery nurse qualifications (NNEB/GNVQ) through work-based placements – in this sense, the crèche has a dual function. All around the building is evidence of the Project's main focus – the repair and restoration of motor vehicles and general engineering. Inside the Project's building, there are classic bikes in the kitchen, Harley Davidson clocks on the walls and posters of scrambling bikes everywhere.

In the yard area of the old Project workshop is the new gardening workshop for residents, and everywhere is an intense buzz of activity, with people purposefully going about their business.

LEARNING A RANGE OF SKILLS AT BRAUNSTONE MOTORCYCLE WORKSHOP

At the top of the building – on the first floor – is the administrative hub of the Project. A small team of administrative staff, outreach workers and project managers write applications and monitor and evaluate service delivery for the many organisations that provide funding to support projects such as:

Legal Buzz: the 'Legal Buzz' Community Training Programme, which gained £589,897 of funding from New Deal for Communities to supply training and youth activities until March 2006, includes the opening of two workshops.

Learn-Tech Youth Training Programme: this course is run over a 75-hour and 12-week period and is intended to provide young people with good background knowledge of basic motorcycle mechanics and other learning opportunities, while continuing to offer them training in life skills.

Mech Start Adult Training Programme: this is a course designed to provide unemployed people with a head start towards getting a job in car industry. It provides training in relevant 'hands-on' skills and other qualifications that will help them gain employment.

'On Two Wheels' Motor Cycle Awareness Programme: this is an initiative of Youth Clubs

UK, which is supported by the Department of Transport, Kawasaki Motorcycles and the Royal Automobile Club (RAC).

A five-minute drive to an adjacent part of the estate revealed a different face to Braunstone – one with complete streets and culs-de-sac full of empty properties and bungalows with overgrown gardens and thick, rusty, perforated steel plates boarding up windows and doors. It also demonstrated a number of possibilities. The four streets we passed, for example, soon will be purchased through the Braunstone New Deal for Communities and will be put to good use as homes and as resource and advisory centres. There are also existing resource and community centres as well as an early years' centre and an agreed Sure Start initiative for the area.

Driving past the park, I made my way, with Wayne, to the Brailsford Industrial Estate to see physical proof of the work of the New Deal for Communities. I visited two recently opened workshops – both of which demonstrated innovation as well as hope for the people of Braunstone.

Motorcycle workshop

A range of activities takes place in the Project's motorcycle workshop. A number of residents from Leicester have donated motorcycles for restoration, and a number of antique bikes have been restored to their former glory. Young people on the estate have restored pre-1920s motorcycles by enamelling fuel tanks, chroming bumpers and polishing cylinder fins – as well as actually getting the engines to work. The work carried out in the workshop has featured in specialist motorcycle magazines such as The Classic Motorcycle, and enthusiasts from various parts of the UK and Europe – after seeing the quality and skill with which the Project's young people restore classic bikes – gladly paid for specialist restoration work.

Through their work on classic and modern bikes, young adults learn a whole range of specialist skills – not just in terms of repairing and restoring motorbikes, but also in cooperation, team building and planning. Their confidence is boosted, and work on numeracy, literacy and life skills back in the classroom helps them apply new skills in maths and English in a very practical way. The individual case studies of young adults that have benefited from various Project initiatives speak for themselves:

RF is a 27-year-old man from the New Parks Estate who has learning difficulties and is currently unemployed. He has completed his Open College Network (OCN) Level 1 in Mechanics, gained a first-aid certificate, completed Compulsory Basic Training and a Full Motorbike test, has finished doing his Theory Test Training and will soon take his Theory Test.

BB is a 25-year-old man from Braunstone who has a son that uses our crèche facility. He is currently unemployed, but he has completed his OCN Level 1 in Mechanics.

NM is a 22-year-old woman from Braunstone who left education at the age of 15 and is currently in part-time employment. She has completed her OCN Level 1 in Mechanics, gained a first-aid certificate, finished doing her Theory Test Training and will soon take her Theory Test.

The same determination, energy, enjoyment and personal satisfaction were demonstrated in the adjacent engineering workshop, where young adults were learning new skills in design, metal manipulation and paint spraying.

THE FUTURE FOR BRAUNSTONE

I left Braunstone with a feeling that many developments still needed to take place before the area could truly be turned around – there was still unemployment, burnt-out cars in the park and, of course the boarded up houses. But there was also energy and optimism in Braunstone, a significant investment in adults and an understanding of the importance of their learning and how this contributes towards the regeneration of communities.

Braunstone Estate in Leicester

-7-

ADULT AND

COMMUNITY LEARNING,

NEIGHBOURHOOD

RENEWAL

AND THE ECONOMY

EDUCATION AND LIFELONG LEARNING SERVICE
Working in partnership

> *Labour market strategy must...overcome the obstacles to entry to the labour market facing disadvantaged people, including people from black and minority ethnic backgrounds and from low employment neighbourhoods – above all, by providing effective support for people without jobs who currently lack skills and aptitudes to compete effectively for work, and by forging effective partnerships with business.*
>
> **POLICY ACTION TEAM 1 – JOBS 2000**

INTRODUCTION

Reversing years of neighbourhood decline requires long-term investment and new ways of working. For the government, two important new ways of working are to ensure that initiatives to tackle poverty and reduce the gap between the poor and the rest of population are joined up and to ensure that such connections are made through partnerships.

As far as the government is concerned, local strategic partnerships bring together the different parts of the public, private and voluntary community sectors so that initiatives and services support rather than contradict each other. The business sector has a particularly important role to play in the regeneration of communities.

Although businesses usually are established for the purpose of making profits, engaging with communities and making a conscious effort to support local regeneration can often serve a range of interests – as a recent initiative involving a number of partners in Liverpool demonstrated.

WORKING WITH THE BUSINESS SECTOR

In 2001, the Liverpool Education and Lifelong Learning Service worked in partnership with a local Jobs Education and Training (JET) Service, the Job Bank, Career Decisions, the Job Centre and ASDA to provide a two-day application and interview preparation course for local residents in a deprived area of Liverpool. The course was intended for people interested in applying for 350 jobs on offer at a new ASDA store to be built on Smithdown Road in Liverpool. Six courses were set up at two venues in the area, and 100 local people attended the courses.

The process

I met with Andy Parkinson, guidance officer for the Adult Learning Service in Liverpool's Education Directorate, to disentangle a fairly complex story about working in partnership, economic development and preparing people from local communities to take advantage of new job opportunities.

The newly established JET Service was based in Job Bank's building in the Kensington area of Liverpool. Job Bank provides a range of services for local people, including information about job and training opportunities. Job Bank arranged for ASDA staff to be based there for a four- to five-month period before the store opened. This arrangement was critical to the success of the venture, in that it helped cement relationships between the ASDA staff and the staff of Job Bank, JET, Lifelong Learning Service and Employment Service who coordinated all aspects of the recruitment campaign.

The prelude to building the ASDA store had been long, with a significant amount of money spent on preparing the land after the demolition of a hospital. Preparation also included a

LYNNE DEBBAZIE (BUSINESS SUPPORT MANAGER) AND SUCCESSFUL TRAINEES AT ASDA

major resurfacing of Smithdown Road. Over a period of several months, almost two miles of road was resurfaced. Everyone waited in anticipation for the opening up of the biggest superstore in the community, which was scheduled for December 2001, and wondered whether they would be able to afford to shop there.

In anticipation of the need for people to work in ASDA, workers at Job Bank, through the JET Service, decided to find out what ASDA would be looking for from job applicants in terms of skills and competencies. A presentation was arranged at the Job Bank to give ASDA's personnel and training section an opportunity to explain their interview procedure and indicate exactly what they would be looking for in candidates. This was to enable Job Bank staff, in conjunction with trainers from Liverpool Education Department's Adult Learning Service, to prepare local people for interviews.

Once staff members were clear about what ASDA required, they set about devising a training programme. When the training programme was ready, training opportunities were advertised in the local newspaper. All courses were to be provided free of charge for anyone who wanted to take advantage of them.

The training

According to Policy Action Team 1 – Jobs 2000:

> **There is an unequal distribution of the skills and aptitudes which employers want; long-term joblessness undermines self-confidence, interpersonal skills and work record to which employers attach importance, or prevents young people from acquiring them in the first place.**

The response to the training was overwhelming, with the demand for places outstripping the number of places available. The programme was put together based on the thorough knowledge of what ASDA was looking for in successful candidates. The programme also tackled the kind of issues that potential job applicants would be concerned about, such as how gaining employment would effect benefit entitlement and their employment rights.

A carefully thought out programme was presented over a two-day period and included the following elements:

- What ASDA wants: this part of the course was presented by ASDA staff. ASDA's recruitment process was explained as well as rates of pay, benefits and what ASDA looks for in job applicants.

- Benefit entitlement check: a financial advice worker from Liverpool Education Department's Lifelong Learning Service arranged one-to-one benefit checks for trainees who needed advice on benefit entitlement. This gave trainees an opportunity to assess whether applying for jobs would be worthwhile financially.

- Effective application techniques: this involved an in-depth look at the ASDA application form, a discussion on what makes a good application and an explanation of the scoring system for individual questions. Trainees were given copies of application forms so they could produce draft applications.

- References: guidance was given on the choice of suitable referees.

On the second day of the course, trainees were given feedback on their draft application forms, their scores were explained and they were given advice on how to improve their performance. Trainees were also given the opportunity to complete application forms with one-to-one support from tutors and guidance workers.

The final part of the course focused on the interview and included mock interviews on a one-to-one basis. All trainees who completed the course were ready to apply for the various job opportunities available at ASDA.

The success of the course

ASDA sent out 5,000 application forms, of which approximately 1,500 were returned, and it was easily able to recruit the 350 staff needed for its new superstore. This partnership had produced the best response ASDA had ever had for positions to a new store and the quality of applications had been exceptional, with 80 per cent of applicants going through to the second stage of the interview process – group interviews. ASDA's average matriculation to the second interview stage is 20 per cent. Personnel officers later explained to Job Bank staff that they happily could have recruited 800 people had there been 800 jobs.

After the course

Staff at Job Bank quickly recognised that something needed to be done with the people who were not successful in their applications to ASDA, particularly knowing that so many local people were looking for part-time and full-time work. The local JET Service, through the Job Bank, and Lifelong Learning staff set up a further range of courses designed to help people update or learn new job-related skills and increase their employability.

These new training opportunities were offered after further discussions with ASDA. A letter was written to its head office explaining the need for further training and suggesting there could be a way of working directly with all those who had applied for jobs at ASDA. This was clearly a group of people seeking gainful employment and further training opportunities would serve a range of purposes for all partners.

For ASDA, it would show the caring aspect of their organisation, which wished to support applicants further in their endeavours to secure employment. For the applicants, there was the benefit of additional training. For the training services, it was an opportunity to engage more people in training. A letter and various training programmes were sent to the 1,500 people who had completed application forms.

The Job Bank provided space for a range of courses that ran from January to March 2002. These courses were offered free of charge and were supported through the European Social Fund, as part of a project called Community Campus. Overall, 114 people took advantage of courses, some enrolling on several. Some of the courses on offer were certificated, such as the Health and Safety course. The full range of courses offered included an introduction to information technology, food hygiene, customer care, computer literacy and English for work. These courses proved to be very successful and are to be offered from Job Bank on a permanent basis.

Partnerships and neighbourhood renewal

This partnership initiative shows how adult and community learning, linked to the needs of local business, can contribute towards neighbourhood renewal and help a local area to improve the environment, reduce worklessness and improve levels of educational attainment. The ASDA store on Smithdown Road has a very local flavour. It is set in an area with a significant number of people who are black and from minority groups, and people from these groups are well reflected within the workforce.

The community gains direct economic benefit from local people being employed in any business or service. Spending power provides local people with choices – in this case, a choice about where to spend money. Spending money in the local community of Smithdown Road provides opportunities for the establishment of new services to meet new demands. Of course, the 350 new employees at ASDA can't make a significant impact alone, but a significant impact could be made if more existing businesses worked in partnership with education services and community-based initiatives and recognised the potential of adult and community learning in regenerating communities.

FUTURE PLANS

The partnership with ASDA was seen very much as a pilot project for the staff of JET Services. Lynne Debbazie, business support manager, informed me that JET, with the same partners,

THE JOB BANK, KENSINGTON

intends to work with new employers as they come into the area. Prime examples are Tesco and Matalan: both companies are building major stores in the Eastern Link (cluster partnership) area, and partners are already going through the same processes – establishing what employers want and familiarising themselves with the unique nature of their recruitment and selection procedures. Lynne explained:

> **It's all about customised training and finding out what employers are looking for in an applicant. Once a local person is successful in securing employment, other opportunities often follow. As with ASDA, for example – they offer fantastic training opportunities, they very rarely offer jobs, they employ from within, they have management training programme and various work-based training packages at NVQ level.**

The local residents who were unsuccessful in getting jobs at ASDA, but who took advantage of further training through Job Bank, were contacted and informed of a series of Tesco open days. Job Bank personally contacted 314 people by phone. JET staff also went to the open days to get an insight into what Tesco were looking for – and so the cycle began again. Tesco opened on Saturday 14 September 2002 with 304 available jobs. Unofficial figures estimate that over 50 per cent of the successful candidates were offered jobs because of the training offered by Job Bank. Matalan opened in the Kensington area on 17 October 2002 with 120 available jobs.

The team at Job Bank and their partners are exploring new areas for training for local people in technology. Partners keep open an ever-watchful eye, so as to be well informed of new developments and employer requirements and well placed to prepare local residents.

Education
and Lifelong
Learning
Service

KNITWEAR, FOOTWEAR AND APPAREL TRADES (KFAT)
Providing language support in the workplace

> People who live in areas that suffer from severe social disadvantage are disproportionately likely to have few or no qualifications, poor literacy and numeracy skills, and low self-confidence and 'coping' skills. Low levels of qualifications and skills do not only mean that people are more likely to be unemployed and hence poor. Low skill levels have a sapping effect on people's self-confidence and they also reduce an individual's capacity – and willingness – to act.
>
> POLICY ACTION TEAM 2 – SKILLS, 2000

COMMUNITY REGENERATION THROUGH EDUCATION

MANCHESTER ADULT EDUCATION SERVICE (MAES) recently underwent significant reorganisation. This has meant a range of changes to the physical locations in which adults learn, a close examination of the nature of its education provision to adults and a detailed analysis of who uses which services.

The services that MAES delivers are based on intelligence, the gathering of ward data and consultation with learners in order to assess their needs and experiences. MAES is dedicated to reaching its strategic objectives, which include raising the participation of adults in education, learning and training, and increasing demand for learning by adults. Ultimately, MAES aims to:

raise participation and achievement through delivery of high quality learning and training programmes and activities, which puts the learner at the heart of everything we do...
(Adult Learning Plan, March 2002)

...within a framework of equality of opportunity and sharing the Government's vision of...

...a learning society in which everyone has the opportunity to go as far as their talents and efforts take them. MAES will provide accessible, high quality, locally delivered opportunities that meet the needs of the diverse communities of Manchester...To this end we will champion equality of opportunity [and] widen participation for adults who are currently underrepresented in MAES.
(Equal Opportunities Policy, May 2002)

ESOL in the Workplace (Knitwear) Project

The ESOL (English for Speakers of Other Languages) in the Workplace (Knitwear) Project is a prime example of innovation, partnership, outreach and research, as well as of the role of education in the regeneration of communities. I met with MAES project manager, Eamonn Graal, to find out more about the KFAT initiative. It is evident that the Project improves an adult's ability to do a job, while at the same time broadening horizons and providing a springboard into new opportunities. It is an example of how MAES, by operating in partnership, is working towards a learning society in Manchester and providing learning opportunities in the workplace for a hard-to-reach group of non-traditional learners.

The Project is an extension of work initiated two years ago. MAES worked with the Textiles Department at the University of Manchester Institute of Science and Technology (UMIST), the KFAT Union, the Basic Skills Agency, the Knitwear Association (Employers) and the Trade Union Learning Service to deliver two phases of ESOL programmes to learners recruited from seven factories in the Ardwick area of Manchester. Some 40 students were taught in ten-week blocks and received certificates from the Greater Manchester Open College Network.

The Textile Department of UMIST had successfully bid for £3.5 million from the Equal Fund for a three-and-a-half year project. The ambitions of this Project and its aims are radical and wide-ranging. The overall aim is to reverse the decline in the knitwear and textiles industry in Manchester, form 'clusters' of five factories each and embark on a wide-ranging programme of training of staff – from workers to managers. The training consists of a number of elements: management technique and approach, computer systems, work-life balance and ESOL.

The knitwear industry is mainly staffed by second-language speakers – from operatives to managers. This being the case, ESOL was identified as central to the success of the entire Project. The lack of basic English skills had proved a barrier to the life chances of workers in the industry and to productivity and efficiency.

The infrastructure for partnership had already been developed and was a continuation of MAES's already good work. As a pilot 'introduction' to the major programmes planned under the auspices of the Equal fund, a ten-week programme of learning was organised for April, May and June 2002. The Trade Union Learning Service committed to funding the Project's incidentals, such as materials and enrolment fees, and MAES used conventional funding from the Learning and Skills Council to support the courses. MAES set up five classes a week (5.30–7.30pm daily), which were taught by one full-time tutor and two part-time tutors.

MAES's contacts with the Textile Department of UMIST and the knitwear industry made it possible for the courses to take place in the learning suite above a manufacturing base in a geographically central area of Ardwick – a location that would maximise participation. The Textile Department of UMIST produced a publicity leaflet and employed a temporary project worker to recruit learners from the 25 factories local to Ardwick.

The introductory programme aimed to 'test the waters' of learner readiness and willingness and to build relations between project worker, tutors and learners, in the hope that individual learners would become advocates for the Project. The ten-week 'pilot' was a bridge between the work two years earlier and the proposed work to be funded by Equal and named 'Textile Advanced Skills' or 'TASk'.

Who are the learners?

The ten-week programme originally was intended for employees working in the local knitwear industry. These people are traditionally excluded from learning and have no access to language provision because of their work pattern and family commitments. The Trade Union Learning Service stated, however, that no impediment exists to non-workers participating. The initial public-

Knitwear, Footwear and Apparel Trades (KFAT)

ity targeted retail outlets, mosques and libraries as well as factories, and at the time of writing, about five participants were not employed in the knitwear industry.

After a leaflet translated into Punjabi and Bengali was sent to 25 local factories, the temporary project worker employed by UMIST went into the factories to talk to the employers and groups of employees. Success in recruiting learners can be attributed, in large part, to the long-standing relationship the project worker has had with employers in the industry.

Course content

The ten-week introductory course is non-accredited. In keeping with MAES's policy, the tutor and participants engage in initial negotiations over the content of the programme. Scope within a whole-class programme is also given to individual learning goals. Eamonn Graal, project manager, explains:

KNITWEAR INDUSTRY WORKERS HAVE MISSED OUT ON LEARNING

The balance of language acquisition and confidence building is about equal in a programme of learning like this. Learners were asked in what situations they felt more confident (as the course had progressed) and their confidence-level has exactly matched the kinds of topics and situations we have been delivering. This is not 'scientifically' measurable against, say, grammatical improvement, but is a qualitative shift in self-perception.

MAES has a set procedure of programme negotiation. For the first course, the learners were asked whether they wished to learn language for work or language that they would find useful outside of work. The learners opted for the latter. Tutors then asked the learners what situations they found themselves in that required English. Their answers resulted in the decision to concentrate on the dominant skills of speaking and listening, because the ten-week course would not be sufficient to concentrate on reading and writing skills.

A nine-week programme of work was drafted around situations and topics decided by the students: health, job seeking, housing, legal, shopping and travel. Within this functional programme, whole arrays of grammatical issues emerged and were responded to. The classes included learners of mixed ability, so the tutors adapted their material to suit the different levels of the class.

Two students asked about their progress commented that in two situations that week they had felt better able to communicate and to engage in the process of using the English language.

Project monitoring

MAES has an end-of-course evaluation procedure, in which students are asked in detail about how they think they faired. Longer courses require a system of six-weekly assessments, but this was not appropriate because of the short-term nature of the programme.

Eamonn currently is writing a detailed evaluation of the programme that will also incorporate the views of managers. This is in close keeping with MAES's aim of listening to learners, finding out what they want and about their experiences, and basing future service provision on the knowledge gained.

The Project and neighbourhood renewal

Eamonn explained:

> **The knitwear industry forms a large part of the economic life of the Ardwick Ward of Manchester. The introductory project and the projected Equal-bid project represent key elements in the retention and renewal of that industry. In addition, information from our enrolment forms indicate that a proportion of the employees we are teaching also lives in Ardwick Ward.**

Knitwear, Footwear and Apparel Trades (KFAT)

MAES uses ward data to plan for future provision. The service already has established from this Project (and from other sources of information) that the area has a substantial population of single, male Afghani asylum seekers and refugees. This information will be used to rationalise Manchester's adult education provision and match curriculum delivery to community needs.

This introductory and pilot programme was organised to set the scene for a much broader and sustainable project as part of a bid for funding from the Equal Fund. The Project is designed to involve 100 learners over a three-year period, all of whom will be working in the industry. The Project has already brought together 15 partners, with MAES at the heart of ESOL provision. It is being monitored by IAGO European Consultants and managed by the project worker based at UMIST.

The implications for neighbourhood renewal in the scope of this Project are far-reaching and significant. The introductory course should be seen in the light of this long-term plan.

Through a variety of initiatives, MAES and its partners have worked successfully with hard-to reach learners by providing services in the workplace or in centres that are safe and convenient. These initiatives aim to support workers and managers in the knitwear industry, so that they are able to work more effectively and increase both the production and quality of their garments.

By helping learners acquire or improve their English language skills, KFAT is providing a basic building block essential to successful employment. The KFAT initiative may also have broadened the horizons and opportunities of people in the knitwear industry in Manchester.

Learners and entrepreneurs

> 'A shortage of jobs, local services and enterprise is one aspect of exclusion facing people in disadvantaged neighbourhoods. But sustainable neighbourhood renewal will not happen without enterprise development.'
>
> POLICY ACTION TEAM 3 – BUSINESS 2000

SOUTHAMPTON

UNEMPLOYMENT ACROSS SOUTHAMPTON has declined since February 1993, when it reached a peak of 14.7 per cent; this is in line with national trends, which peaked at 10.7 per cent in February 1993. The rate for the city in August 2001 was 2.8 per cent compared with the United Kingdom's average of 3.2 per cent. Only three of the city's wards had unemployment rates higher than the national average; the rates for the two inner city wards – Bargate and St Luke's– were the highest at 7.0 per cent and 4.7 per cent, respectively. In August 2001, the total number of unemployed people in Southampton was 2,875: a decrease of 715 since June 2000.

Although Southampton is not one of the poorest areas in the country, it does have pockets of deprivation that are not necessarily identified through the standard indices of deprivation. Relatively affluent wards include a significant number of households with tenants and owners living on, or below, the poverty line. The following facts and figures provide a snapshot of Southampton:

- The population within a 45-minute drive of Southampton is two million.

- Of these two million, 43 per cent are within the high-spending, 16–44 age group (UK average is 42 per cent) and 58 per cent are white-collar workers (UK average is 56 per cent).

- Of the major centres in the UK, Southampton has the fourth largest catchment population after Manchester, Leeds and Bradford, and Birmingham.

- More than three million people, with an annual retail spending power of over £2.5 billion, live within 60 minutes' drive of Southampton city centre.

- Ford Motor Company, Pratt & Whitney Canada, Russ Berrie, Draper Tools, Meachers and Christian Salvesen all have a significant presence in Southampton.

- Southampton Container Terminal is the only terminal in the UK that offers receipt and delivery of containers transported by road, 24 hours a day, seven days a week.

- Southampton's two freightliner terminals operate 24 hours a day.

Fairbridge
Funky
Furniture

■ The city has a student population of over 31,000.

■ In total, 78 per cent of the economically active population hold an academic or vocational qualification.

■ Southampton Airport is the leading business airport in central, south England.

FAIRBRIDGE

Fairbridge as an organisation began in the early 20th century and has been up and running in its present form since the early 1980s. Fairbridge Solent began life in September 1999. Located in the centre of Southampton, it provides services for a wide range of young people from various parts of the city. The organisation offers many courses for young people including numeracy skills, art, Internet projects, and drama and cooking workshops, as well as a range of outdoor activities, such as kayaking, canoeing, rock climbing, abseiling, white-water rafting and camping.

Fairbridge Solent works with disadvantaged young people who, for one reason or another, have been pushed to the margins of society. Through a wide range of challenging activities it aims to help young people learn the skills they need to meet the opportunities and responsibilities of employment and of life generally. A number of agencies refer young people between the ages of 13 and 25 years, particularly the older young people (16–25 years), to Fairbridge Solent. These agencies include the probation service, homeless hostels, and drug rehabilitation and mental health services.

FAIRBRIDGE FUNKY FURNITURE PROJECT

The link between furniture restoration and neighbourhood renewal may not be immediately obvious, but on closer examination, the skills and new knowledge and information that young people gain through the Fairbridge Funky Furniture Project make them better placed to participate in employment and training opportunities within their local area and this has an impact on community regeneration.

The Project runs courses for six weeks, four times a year and is scheduled to run for two years. The activities on each course involve site visits to factories, museums and antique shops, which give young people ideas and inspiration for work they will do on two pieces of furniture – one item is sold and the other they keep. A typical programme for a funky furniture course usually involves the group first getting to know each other and setting ground rules between members and setting aims for themselves – what they want to achieve in each session and by the end of the course. The aims can be anything from 'being patient' and 'learning to work with others' to 'creating an attractive piece of furniture', which they may have never have attempted before. Dawn Parker from the furniture project explains:

> **During the planning stages, Fairbridge staff also take out the young people on visits to antique shops and museums for ideas of designs for their pieces. They then move onto the actual planning of their pieces of furniture, which they make notes of each week of their progression. They begin with a blank undecorated box for example and plan what they would like to do with it i.e. what colour and design, and how they are going to do it. Next is the practical stage, which continues until the end of the course, when they have completed their piece. Once the participants have finished both pieces of furniture, they are presented certificates at a completion ceremony and are allotted a day in which they will take their 'Funky Furniture' to market to sell to the general public.**

Through the Project, young people learn the importance of valuing the environment through recycling items of furniture that have been discarded. Participation not only helps young people learn the art of renovating and recycling old furniture and technical skills in basic carpentry and decorating but also the business and marketing skills needed to sell the furniture they have restored. In addition, the Project also facilitates development of personal skills, such as perseverance and dedication in working towards achieving goals

The first course has already been completed successfully. Fairbridge Solent aims to have 25 young people between the ages of 16 and 25 to complete a course per year.

Where the participants move to after the Funky Furniture Project is different for every individual because of their hectic social lives, but most stay involved with Fairbridge while they actively seek work. The Project has proved extremely beneficial in building key skills for young people involved – from a sense of fulfilment and achievement, which some may never have felt before, to learning to be patient and tolerant towards others. This is essential when working within a group twice a week for six weeks, six hours a day. The practical skills in art and design have proved immensely valuable for learners' personal experiences and on their curriculum vitae.

OLD FURNITURE GETS THE FAIRBRIDGE RESTORATION TREATMENT.

Our learners

The Fairbridge programme is so successful because it caters for each individual in the ways that they need. The Fairbridge Funky Furniture Project does this in a very visible way: the learners actually see a piece of work transform in front of them – they create it and the general public can buy it. In addition, their personal and life skills improve while they are taught the practical skills.

Each young person can receive individual support in small groups. This means that every learner's individual needs can be met.

To some extent, learners already have been identified when they are referred to Fairbridge by the various agencies, and they are in need of help provided by Fairbridge. The Project is extra to the general help Fairbridge

Fairbridge
Funky
Furniture

Solent provides, and it encourages young people and learners to participate in something very creative and appealing.

The role of adult and community learning

The young people who participate in the Project do not receive any formal accreditation on completing the course, but they do receive Fairbridge completion certificates at a graduation ceremony – after the first course, the Right Honourable John Denham MP presented the certificates. However, Fairbridge's mission is to give young people the skills they need to meet the opportunities and responsibilities of society today, by offering them a long-term personal development programme that builds confidence, motivation and personal, social and life skills. The Funky Furniture Project is an integral part of this, because it teaches them practical and life skills while working towards a very tangible achievement. This in turn improves their chances of re-entering education or employment and benefits the community by keeping them off the streets and working towards a more positive future.

FAIRBRIDGE DEVELOPS SKILLS IN BOTH DESIGN AND BUSINESS.

Funky philosophy

The Funky Furniture course is not set up to lead to a qualification, being designed rather as the first step for young people, providing them with motivation to pursue formal qualifications or employment. Kevin Allan, Manager of Fairbridge Solent said:

> **The funding of Funky Furniture has allowed us to develop something we know works into a substantial course for young people. The benefit of the programme is clear to see from both the quality of the work produced and the commitment of the participants.**

Tutor Rebecca Bennett said:

> **It has been great working with the young people on the Funky Furniture course. The enthusiasm and motivation for their work is clear to see and very encouraging. This course gives them something very solid to work towards – a clear achievement.**

The experience for young people on the project is very rewarding, one young person commented:

> **I completed the Funky Furniture course a few weeks ago now, but I loved it. I really enjoyed getting to make the boring pieces of furniture look nice and to get to keep one myself was even better! It gave me something to work towards.**

Project monitoring

The evaluation techniques used for the Funky Furniture project are mainly anecdotal – the young people evaluate how well they feel they have done after each session, and once the course is completed they evaluate how well they think they have done overall: whether they are pleased with the finished pieces or not, what they would have changed, and so on. This is essentially what Fairbridge is about – helping young people to learn through their own personal experience and to evaluate how they have done and what they would change.

The evidence of how successful the project is lies in the quality of the finished products and the ongoing development of the young people within the Fairbridge programme as a whole. The young people themselves, and how they feel about their finished pieces, measure the 'evidence in quality'. The pieces are extremely sellable, however, and are sold at the local market, which demonstrates that they are of a general high quality.

THE FAIRBRIDGE MISSION

The Fairbridge mission is to provide help and support to young people in the area who need it most. In doing this, Fairbridge can help neighbourhood renewal by taking young people off the streets, away from criminal activities and negative behaviour, and directing their efforts into something more worthwhile. The Project not only has the potential to impact on crime reduction targets for the area but also on aspirations for improving the local environment through recycling and improving the employment prospects of the disaffected young.

Fairbridge
Funky
Furniture

-8-

SEAFARING

AND

NEIGHBOURHOOD

RENEWAL

FLAGSHIP PROJECT
A collective
identity

'In the nineteenth century, Liverpool was the international capital of the great-est era of sail achievement. It was a tough, tough trade to live and work in. The personal qualities and tenacity which working under sail developed in seafarers fed back into their families and communities to develop a unique resource of personal resilience, humour in adversity and determi-nation to achieve. The last frontier – the sea – is still waiting outside the Mersey harbour wall; the Flagship Project is maintaining access to it for local people – one might say 'ordinary local people', but we're finding that given a big challenge and the opportunity to achieve it, no-one is ordinary.'

SUSAN HANLEY-PLACE, CHIEF EXECUTIVE OF MERSEY HERITAGE

THE FLAGSHIP PROJECT
Neighbourhood renewal and a sense of community identity

NEIGHBOURHOOD RENEWAL usually is thought of in terms of community centres, economic re-engagement and environmental improvements. A fundamental issue, however, is that of community identity – an area on which the Mersey Heritage Trust in Liverpool places signifi-cant emphasis.

The Trust runs an award-winning Training and Learning Project funded principally by the Adult and Community Learning Fund, which is rebuilding a historic square-rigged tall ship to act as a Community Flagship for Merseyside. Work on the Flagship is well advanced and has earned distinctive praise – not only within the field of community education, but also from experts in the world of tall ships.

From relatively simple beginnings in January 2000 – teaching woodwork skills that enabled learners to carry out work like refurbishing hatches and laying in a new lower deck – the Project's scope and achievements have progressed to a complete rebuild of the ship's complex rig, taking down and rebuilding masts and spars, and setting up traditional rigging to quality stan-dards.

The crucial point is that all the Project's work is done by the learners themselves; they work as a learning team that encompasses a very wide range of people. Everyone contributes

Flagship
Project

to the overall achievement by using the best of their abilities, which are constantly stretched to new levels.

Project leader Geoff Hanley, who took early retirement from P&O Ferrymasters to lead the Project and won a National Adult Tutor of the Year Award in 2001, said:

> We originally assumed we would bring in outside experts on a regular basis, particularly to teach our team about traditional rigging. Most traditional ship rebuilds rely on bringing in experts for whom local volunteers do labouring, but we soon decided our learners were going to become the experts themselves, researching and practicing the old skills of square-rig and filling-out, understanding how it works, until they could rebuild the rig to certification standards. We wanted to encourage ownership – and now it's 100 per cent.

In the nineteenth century, Liverpool was one of the greatest ports in the world – an identity that forged the city's consciousness as 'a cosmopolitan seaport through which the tides of the world flowed'. Mersey Heritage's chief executive, Susan Hanley-Place MBE, commented:

> The last decade's flurry of grant-aided revitalisation initiatives on Merseyside has not on the whole taken into account the way in which community identity influences grassroots commitment to neighbourhood renewal.

Aims and objectives

The Flagship Project was established to provide members of the Merseyside community with an opportunity to become centrally involved in the rebuilding and subsequent operation of a distinguished square-rigged sailing ship. The ship, the ZEBU, is designated as a Community Flagship and will be involved in a seagoing educational programme out of Liverpool.

The Flagship Project provides volunteers with a training and learning programme based on the seafaring heritage of Merseyside. It focuses on four main areas:

- Acquisition of new skills or redeployment of existing skills to help volunteers identify new training and employment directions.

- Activating learning potential in participants who have not taken up adult learning for a variety of reasons, including the inappropriateness of existing lifelong learning provision.

- Building confidence, teamworking capacity and commitment to finding new life directions among the volunteer team.

- Rebuilding connections between the generations, so that young people can learn from older people and seniors can find new mentoring roles within a diverse and equal Project community.

Beneficiaries

The Project has always aimed to draw in as diverse a group of learners as possible, representing a cross section of the Merseyside community and outreaching into Cheshire and Lancashire. From the outset, the organisers expected the Project to appeal particularly to people who are under-represented in lifelong learning provision – older men from traditional trade backgrounds, young people who have not achieved at school and unemployed people looking for a change of direction. Most participants fall into these broad categories, but the Project has also

TEAMWORK – ESSENTIAL ON THE ZEBU

recruited some participants with learning and physical disabilities and with distinctive social problems, mixing them in effectively with the more advantaged members of the group.

The role of adult and community learning in the Project

Because of the very varied abilities and aspirations of the learners, the Flagship Project encompasses a very broad mix of informal and formal learning. At one end of the scale are the Project's newly-graduated offshore yacht-masters; at the other end are teenagers learning painting and working aloft. While learning the practical skills, the participants also learn that the ability to work in a team and to develop confidence and a commitment to work are important skills. As Susan explains:

> Some of the team have developed top-class professional tall ship rigging skills, and working alongside them might be a person with learning difficulties for whom wood-turning, belaying pins, serving rigging shrouds and working 30 feet aloft blacking-down the rigging rank amongst his best-ever learning achievements.

What happens on the ZEBU?

The Flagship Project offers a very diverse curriculum. Susan and colleagues counted up to 50 substantial learning strands in the first year of the project; the second year added more than 20 more. For example, learning strands in relation to refurbishing all the ship's pulley blocks include:

Flagship
Project

SETTING UP THE RIG

- practical learning about wood conservation

- theoretical learning about how the blocks work (a learning strand that is about practical physics and engineering concepts, which is delivered mainly through hands-on experiential learning and textbooks)

- acquiring a transferable trade skill by practicing a substantial amount of block conservation and restoration (this involves putting the core skills and theoretical understanding together to evolve a competency that encompasses mechanics, conservation and woodworking and that equips the learner with specific skills and the confidence and ability to apply them in other equally unfamiliar areas).

Susan further explained that:

> The Team Project to replace the ship's standing rigging was a very complex group of learning strands leading to an outstanding professional achievement. Team members who undertook the whole project have effectively worked through an entire 'syllabus' in traditional ships' rigging comparable to a City & Guilds or advanced grade NVQ [course].

A substantial number of learning strands involved research to understand the working of traditional ships' rigging. The team used textbooks about 19th century ships' rigs, worked aloft on the Cutty Sark and other tall ships and consulted archival sources. This was informal learning, in that it was not conducted in a classroom with note-taking and written work, but it also was an advanced form of problem-based and experiential learning.

Trainees acquired in excess of 20 skills to professional level. These started with learning how to serve a wire and progressed through the gamut of rigger's skills, such as forming racking seizings, calculating rigging loadings and assembling lanyards, martingales and rigging stays. The culmination of the learning process was the assembly of the rig to seagoing specifications by manipulating the mass of triangles of forces to achieve the correct jib – the boom steeve, mast rake, shroud and stay tensions. Raking back a 72-foot mast by two degrees in an afternoon was no mean team achievement, and when the ship eventually sets sail, crewed by the people who built the rig, the sense of ownership of the technology will be immense. No apologies are made for technical terminology here – the new rig is state-of-the-art 19th-century wind technology.

MONITORING AND EVALUATION

The Project took an innovative approach to monitoring and evaluation. From the outset, most participants clearly were not interested in a project that involved paperwork. They had a variety of good reasons for this, and these were respected. Many of the participants on the Project were unemployed people who had been sent on training courses they described as useless; others were retired people who did not see the Project as adult education but as a means to contribute. Susan described the innovative ways in which the project was monitored and evaluated.

> **We started out with a paperwork system and found it counter-productive. Sitting down to write about 'what I have learned today' was a total turn-off; so was having the project leader write progress notes about them as if they were schoolchildren. We asked everyone to fill in a survey form, and while the comments they made were interesting, we realised some did not like information gathering, and others would struggle to express themselves in writing.**

> **These were not a client group of 'disadvantaged people' – they were a representative cross section of the person-in-the-street, and they just didn't fancy paperwork. They wanted to get on with the work and learn the skills, so we devised a way to achieve effective monitoring without filling a filing cabinet with paper.**

The essential documentation tool for the project became the digital camera. The project leader ensured that every stage of the Project's work was documented by recording involvement, developing skills and the achievements of both teams and individuals. Catching everything on camera soon became part of the Project's culture, and as the camera was passed round the team, learner-led perspectives increasingly featured. A second camera later was used by the team to capture anecdotal moments and personal milestones in greater detail and to archive different features of the Project's progress.

Flagship
Project

A minidisc recorder was also used to record group discussions about their experiences and learning on the Project. This produced some remarkably perceptive observations about the learning process, as well as some very moving statements about how participants' lives were changing. Often the participants least likely to sit down and put their thoughts on paper were the most vocal in expressing how the Project was altering their perspective.

Presentations, which could be run on computers or circulated as hard copy, were drawn up from this evidence. These were the principal medium by which outside organisations evaluated the effectiveness of the Project.

Although the project is moving into a situation where 'hard outcomes' can be identified, the focus of the Project is still its impact on the aspirations and achievements of individuals. The presentations give equal weight to personal development outcomes and skills development and provide cogent evidence of 'soft outcomes'.

COMMUNITY RENEWAL

Geoff Hanley reflected on the Flagship's growing symbolism for community renewal.

> One of our trainees, a young mother of 19, said to me recently 'everyone round where we live is talking about the ZEBU now', and at first I wondered how. Then we thought about all the grandfathers and great-grandfathers who went to sea in Liverpool's tall ships and are still family heroes, and you can start to see that it is still a real community identity. We feel that ourselves – we are a very diverse group, but the ship cloaks us all in her identity; where we all stand is within the ship, and we always have that common identity no matter how diverse we are. Liverpool is a diverse community; every one of the great varieties of nationalities represented here has its origins in seafaring. So it hardly would be surprising for the rebuilding of a square-rigger in the heart of the city to be somewhat symbolic.

> As the ship has been re-rigged – especially recently, when we've finally brought the rebuilt masts and big square-sail spars out of the workshop and set them up on the ship – we've realised that dozens of Merseyside families have been quietly coming to watch the progress week by week. We sometimes overhear them telling visitors about 'their' ship and see them sitting on the benches on the quay nodding their approval. It's quite awesome really – ZEBU is becoming a symbol of the kind of 'neighbourhood regeneration' Liverpool people feel the need to see – not least because it's being done by people like them, on behalf of everyone.

-9-

COMMUNITY

ACTIVISTS

Regeneration fat cats

> 'Relatively few civil servants involved in policy development or programme management have significant first-hand experience of living or working in disadvantaged neighbourhoods. Interchange and secondment activity can provide invaluable development opportunities and lead to better policies and more sensitive management.'
>
> **REPORT OF POLICY ACTION TEAM 16: LEARNING LESSONS**

MIKE LANE is a self-taught community activist who was born and raised in Liverpool; he is a resident of the Kensington area – one of the poorest areas in the country. Learning about the methods and theories of writers such as Paulo Freire and Ira Shor provided Mike with the inspiration needed to take action.

Mike's action comes out of his concerns about developments in his local community. His preferred method of direct action is saturation leafleting. This involves the in-house desktop publishing of thousands of leaflets, which are social commentaries on, among other things, Kensington New Deal for Communities (NDC). These leaflets are distributed in and around the community. He also likes getting out into the streets, on foot and by car, to inform people of his concerns about regeneration through a loud hailer. In this account, he details his concerns.

WHO ARE THE REGENERATION FAT CATS?

These are a bunch of people who are quite incompetent at what they do. The regeneration of Merseyside is creating a job bonanza for these well-paid bureaucrats. As this web page [www.whistleblower.nstemp.com] grows, you will see who the real winners are when it comes to the regeneration game. At present, many poor areas in Great Britain have been earmarked for regeneration funding, which comes mainly from Central Government and the European Commission. Liverpool and Merseyside has received billions of pounds of regeneration funding and is still in the process of receiving it.

Each regeneration partnership is run by a coordinator or a chief executive who earns in the region of £50,000–£60,000 per year. These people, who are mostly all middl- class, live in the prosperous suburbs. They are, as well as being careerists, quite incapable of understanding the

Mike Lane

culture and social dynamics of poor inner city communities. Liverpool's Kensington NDC community is under the threat of mass demolition. The decision to go ahead with these proposed demolitions was made by the Kensington NDC interim board. Many of the original interim board did not even live in the NDC area.

This major decision was made before the five Citizens Panels were set up, and it was based [on] a couple of one-day drop in advice venues (which were never publicised to the community) and the results of a totally inadequate community consultation questionnaire that never reflected the views or the aspirations of the wider community. In other words, the community was led down the garden path by a handful of middle-class, careerist council officers and community toadies.

We now have a situation in which over 50 per cent of the Kensington NDC community is under the threat of proposed demolition. Although the KR [Kensington Regeneration] team and its board will strenuously deny this, they intend to indulge in what can only be described as social cleansing. They have, in the most subtlest of ways, weaved a web of misinformation and deceitful intentions, which are all geared up to rid the Kensington NDC area of people that they presume are bringing the area down. Over 60 per cent of the houses that the KR intend to demolish are owned by social and private landlords, yet out of the 900 houses that they propose to build, only 139 will be available to rent. This means that a colossal 741 houses will be built for sale. This is an obvious attempt to 'yuppify' the area and bring people with a better socio-earning capacity into the NDC zone (people with vocational skills i.e. middle-class).

Over 60 per cent of people in the NDC area live in rented accommodation, and it is amongst these people that the most disadvantaged and socially excluded live; yet they are going to be disenfranchised from the NDC initiative and in effect ghettoised in other poor areas around the city which are not important to the present city centre regeneration (at this present time, the city centre of Liverpool is having billions spent on it – money that was supposed to go into poor areas of Liverpool).

The Kensington NDC area is right next to the city centre and is integral to the city centre regeneration because the M6 motorway runs onto the M62, which runs onto Edge Lane; Edge Lane runs right through the middle of NDC area. Of course, the KR team and its board deny that people who live in rented accommodation will be moved out of the area and have stated that these people will be re-housed in existing voids (empty houses) within the NDC area, but this is unlikely because many of the houses in these areas will be demolished.

The present homeowners will suffer the worst because they will probably be offered a pittance for their homes and if they do not accept, they will be forced into selling with the threat of compulsory purchase orders being served upon them. The KR team have told them that they can move into the new houses, but the new houses will be sold at the market rate, which will be four or five time more than what they will receive for their old properties. The KR team have told them that they can take up shared ownership [shared equity] in one of the new houses, which will be owned by the KR team or whatever body they choose to elect.

What the NDC community should realise is that the regeneration fat cats are experts at reassuring the community. They know that the community want to believe them so they use the community's blind faith in them as a tool to sway the community into a false sense of security.

Homeowners should be ever vigilant, because if they ease up just for one minute the KR council officers will be in like a shot. The community should take no notice of the KR's insistence that the proposed demolition is only a proposal. Remember, the KR got the £32 million, which has now been increased to £62 million, from Central Government on the strength of the 'housing proposal document'.

A WAY FORWARD FOR LOCAL PARTICIPATION

What is the way forward in ensuring community participation in local decision-making? A further discussion with Mike Lane threw some light on this in relation to active citizenship, community participation and civic responsibility. We discussed some of Mike's ideas for the development of open and democratic neighbourhoods. One of his main interests is in exploring ways of working with local people to develop a sense of civic responsibility; for this, Mike argues that there needs to be radical changes, particularly in relation to methods used to achieve community participation.

Mike has written the following text, with quotes and ideas advocated by libertarians Paulo Freire (particularly from his book *Pedagogy of the oppressed*) and Professor Ira Shor (in *Critical teaching for everyday life*, 1982) in mind. These libertarians were experts at defining the undemocratic, complicated and ambiguous ways in which local government and civil servants can, or should be seen to, operate.

PROPOSAL FOR OPENNESS AND PROCEDURE

It is felt by critical community activists who live in poor areas earmarked for regeneration that regeneration administrators, consultants and outreach workers (many of whom who do not live in the rundown community that they work in) do not have the knowledge, understanding or perspective to work with and for the community in a democratic way.

Below is a suggested draft constitution, which tries to encompass democratic openness and procedure within, for example, a New Deal for Communities area. The constitution tries to fit in with the present methodology that is being fostered in many NDC communities throughout the country. Arguably, if communities were left to their own devices they may be able to develop a much better and fairer way of doing things.

CONSTITUTION FOR A SOCIETY OF OPEN DEMOCRATIC NEIGHBOURHOODS

Within any partnership, one of the main concerns should be for equality for the individual. Each member of any partnership should have equal rights, and these rights should be protected. As

Mike Lane

long as certain interest groups and administrators control process, they will always be in a position of power. Once the power is taken away from these interest groups, equality will be possible for all.

NEW DEAL FOR COMMUNITIES

1 Each neighbourhood within an NDC zone will elect its own community NDC board members to make guidelines for the best interests of the people.

2 The NDC board candidates should be selected by virtue of the democratic process used in local and central government elections and not by community resident associations or panels, so that anyone should be able to run for election as a board member by virtue of obtaining ten signatures from people who live in the area in which they intend to run.

3 The NDC community board members should outnumber the paid professional and elected members on the board by at least four. This is because the paid professional service providers, being professional and conversant in community dynamics, have more ability to put their case across in a more convincing manner than the community members. This unfair advantage will always give the paid professionals an edge over the resident board members.

4 The goal of each of the NDC community board members should be to try to help the community be a better place to live, where equality, freedom and concerns for other[s] is of the highest degree.

5 All NDC board meetings should be open to be observed by the community, irrespective of what issues the board meetings cover.

6 All community members other than the board members should remain as silent observers and should only speak if invited to by the NDC board [chairperson].

7 To avoid undemocratic behaviour, all community resident association and community council meetings should be open to members of the NDC community, irrespective of what part of the community the residents live in.

8 Any resident working for the community, either on a voluntary or paid basis, should consider themselves to be trusted servants and not leaders. They should always work to the understanding that the residents as a whole are greater than a small group of people and, as such, are far better at making decisions collectively, if they are allowed to do so. Trusted servants must learn to trust the people they represent, because trusting the people is an indispensable precondition for lasting change.

9 Projects and initiatives should be put together by the community and not imposed onto them by public sector-led regeneration teams or outreach workers.

10 The use of community referendums, especially for major projects, should be common practice and used to further involve the community as a whole in the decision-making process.

11 All repressive codes of conduct should be discontinued. If there is disagreement, at whatever level, the people involved should try to find out why the aggrieved person or persons are distressed.

12 People within the NDC community should try to work for the common good of everyone and not just for himself or herself.

13 As far as possible, the dividing of the community into many different groups should be avoided and discouraged. Regeneration administrators can use this practice as a tool to control and domesticate the community. These focalised forms of action, by intensifying the focalised way of life of poor people in poor rundown communities, hamper the community from perceiving reality critically and keep them isolated from the problems connected with other people who live in other regeneration areas throughout the UK.

14 Looking at [an] NDC regeneration community as a whole entity should be promoted and encouraged. NDC residents should realise that the NDC community, in its entirety, is in reality a very small area.

15 Any person or persons attending any meeting, i.e. Resident Association (be it in whatever area of an NDC zone), Community Council or any meetings connected with [the] NDC initiative cannot be asked to leave by an individual or individuals, but only by a vote of everyone present at that particular meeting.

16 No community leader or activists should have the right to stop any community member from attending a community meeting, Resident Association or any other group, without first putting the issue to the community members of that group in the presence of the person they are proposing to exclude and asking for a vote.

17 As far as possible, cronyism and the formation of community cliques should be discouraged, and it should be continually pointed out that each resident is part of the wider community.

18 As far as possible, parochial [narrow-minded, territorial] behaviour should be discouraged, because paid professional administrators and their outreach workers can use a community's parochial nature as a further tool to subjugate and domesticate residents, thus giving the paid professionals the opportunity to impose their agenda onto an unsuspecting community.

19 Constructive critical dialogue should not be discouraged but rather promoted as an implement for change. Any situation in which some individuals prevent others from engaging in a regeneration project and in the process of inquiry is one of symbolic violence. The

Mike Lane

means used are not important; to alienate community members from their own decision-making is to change them into objects. Those who have been prevented from expressing their opinions are entitled to reclaim their right, using a democratic process, to speak and prevent the constitution of this dehumanising aggression against them.aggression against them.

20 All community residents should be encouraged to change the environment that they live in, be it in whatever area, rather than adapting themselves to that environment.

21 Communities should abolish the community participation and empowerment methodology that is being imposed upon them. Communities should be allowed to independently devise their own community empowerment methodology, without interference from regeneration teams or outreach workers.

22 Paid workers in regeneration teams or service providers should learn to speak with the community and not to them, as in the authoritarian manner of speaking from the top down. They should provide a service and not get involved in the way in which the community chooses to conduct its empowerment strategy

23 As far as possible, the community should devise its own consultation and research methodology, and they should be paid the going rate for doing this. When trying to ascertain what the community wants, the highest standards of qualitative research methodology should be devised and used by the community.

24 There should be a constant flow of truthful, simple and concise information circulated around any NDC community.

COMMUNITY MEETINGS

All community meetings should be held and organised in the most simple of ways in order to encourage full community participation. Below is a suggested set of rules.

1 All meetings should be held in a circle – people can relate better if they sit in a circle. Everyone can sit where they want. People should be able to sit where they feel most comfortable and not in an assigned seat.

2 People at the meeting should not speak only to the chairperson when they talk, but should be able to speak to everyone or to the person they want to respond to.

3 The chairperson should not think herself or himself responsible for filling up silence in order to keep the conversation going.

4 Meetings should be as informal as possible and it should be permissible for residents and the chairperson, or any paid professional service providers, to talk to each other on a first name basis. Calling each other by first names prevents the development of relationships of superiority and inferiority – whether imagined or real.

5 No one should be forced to say anything. Everyone should have an opportunity to talk at one time or another; the same persons should not be allowed to dominate discussions.

GINA HOLDSWORTH
Bransholme
Motivation Group

> Political and cultural barriers (to community and voluntary activity) include: adverse 'labelling' of communities – e.g. by perceiving groups or areas as problems; the reluctance of agencies and professionals to cede power, thus controlling the agenda and blocking local initiatives; and racism and other forms of discrimination practiced by institutions and individuals both by those charged with providing services and within communities.

POLICY ACTION TEAM 9 – COMMUNITY SELF-HELP, 2000

MY NAME IS GINA HOLDSWORTH

My name is Gina Holdsworth. Today I wear the hat of housewife. I have many hats – mum, wife, friend, participation worker, trainer, poverty commissioner and community representative for the Neighbourhood Renewal Unit Task Force.

Although born in London, I now live on Bransholme Estate in Hull. Bransholme – possibly the largest housing estate in Europe, with a population of 35,000 – is recognised as one of the most deprived areas of the North.

Deprivation is increased by lack of choices, lack of opportunities, lack of communication – lack of probably everything. Bransholme does have plenty of unemployment and one-parent families [and] an enormous rate of those suffering from depression and stress-related illnesses.

Because of its sheer size, Bransholme has a bad reputation, and many experience discrimination just because of their postcode. Often perpetuated by many residents because of lack of self-esteem, this in turn is thought by some to be related to low academic achievement and low expectation in our young people.

Forever being promised solutions has caused the people of Bransholme to become suspicious of officialdom, including social services, and those that are trying to help are often seen as the enemy.

Many residents speak of an overwhelming sense of not being in charge of their own lives. These are good and decent people who constantly fight a war on poverty every single day.

POVERTY

They don't see themselves as poor – they all know someone worse off. They've told me of the humiliation of not being able to earn enough to give their family a decent standard of living, of the shame involved in being trapped on benefits.

But, poverty is not only lack of money, it's also about rights, relationships and the way that people are treated, the way that they see themselves – their loss of dignity. It's about feeling powerless – other people manipulating and moving your life around.

Poverty has many dimensions. Of course money can buy things, but there are issues about the quality of housing, about people's health, about their access to decent education and services, and [about] how people who are unable to participate in what is regarded as the normal life of their community are often excluded from the community.

People have often been told that their greatest misfortune is not to be hungry or unable to read– or even to be without work. The greatest misfortune of all is to know that you count for nothing – to the point where even your suffering is ignored.

BRANSHOLME MOTIVATION

Because of this, about seven years ago, I and a few others created a group called Bransholme Motivation, which welcomed everyone living or working on the estate to come along, be motivated and motivate others. The plan was simple: to create a safe secure atmosphere where people felt comfortable, where they could come along when they wanted, for as long as they wanted, and become involved in activities that they were interested in.

It became a place where people listened to and supported each other; it allowed people to come to terms with their own problems in their own way, on their own terms, in their own time. In this way, we encouraged them to become involved with what was happening on the estate, enabling them to feel part of a community, as well as helping them to discover who they were and the good qualities they possessed. Bransholme Motivation was built on the individual. Let me give you two examples.

Gina
Holdsworth

LESLEY'S STORY

Lesley, a lone parent of 20 [years], moved to Bransholme when Becky, her daughter, was three– with only a small suitcase of clothes and a sofa bed. She found herself isolated and alone, without friends and family support. Lesley's days slowly slipped one into another.Although Becky was well looked after, Lesley began missing meals, losing track of days and, when her hot water system broke down, eventually developed an attitude of 'who cares?' She tried time and again to create a proper home, but in her first two years was burgled 12 times.

As Becky grew, she began to show signs of behaviour problems, but Lesley was too frightened to ask for help. She felt that social services would label her a bad mother and take Becky away.

Lesley became a member of Bransholme Motivation and, with help and support, she began to pull herself and her life back together. There were times when she couldn't face us, and we wouldn't see her for weeks, but then she would return, begin again – each time a step further on.

Her life has become much more ordered now. She has an established routine and is on the final year of a college course. Becky was actually diagnosed as hyperactive and suffering from attention deficit disorder; however, Lesley is confident enough now to seek and ask for the help she needs. She now offers support to parents like herself.

MARY'S STORY

Mary, a strong-willed, independent, positive and very active woman of 60, moved to Bransholme 24 years ago. She had been actively creative with various handicrafts and hobbies. After suffering a stroke, Mary lost the use of her right side and found herself restricted in the amount of activities that she could take part in and felt totally isolated. Like many other residents, her life consisted of getting up in the morning, a trip to the shops and going back to bed again.

She has told me how she felt that her life was over – that she was no use to anyone. She felt old, disabled and useless, and she needed to feel useful and in control of her life again. After several visits to Motivation, we discovered her to possess a wealth of experience and knowledge.

We're not sure if we recruited her or whether it was the other way around – she has been working as a volunteer with us six years. Mary worked three days a week as our shop manager, was a founder of the craft club, an enthusiastic, hard-working member and always part of anything happening within the group.

An active instigator of our Anti-Poverty Project, Mary has become a spokesperson for the disabled and older residents of the estate. She is now a trainer in participatory appraisal and has even [taken] part in a participatory appraisal video (used to develop communities all over the world).

Mary uses her participatory appraisal training to empower and involve others, giving an example of how community involvement and training can enrich and improve lives. No shrinking violet, Mary confidently tells people of her belief in them.

It wasn't long before we began to realise that training, although being successfully offered across the estate, was often aimed at one level – offering basic skills training which neither raised people out of their present situation nor reached the roots that so desperately needed it. There were people so far removed from empowerment and inclusion that for them it was so much safer not to try, than to try and fail; and others – like myself – who craved and desired the opportunity to bring about change.

Local structures failed to meet the needs of people at grassroots level. Yet we, the people at grassroots, were successful at meeting the needs of people beyond the roots. We were able to offer the support, experience and training that enabled many residents to tackle issues that impaired their lives – one by one becoming empowered, forming groups, tackling training, achieving and inspiring others.

The group was extremely successful and in March 2000, only five years on, we were awarded national recognition for a plan to tackle poverty involving:

- a community 'pop-in' to alleviate isolation

- a food co-op[erative] to bring in fresh, affordable fruit and veg[etables]

- a community kitchen where we could teach healthy eating on a budget

- a service area where people could wash and iron, because one of the many facilities Bransholme lacks is a launderette.

SUSTAINABILITY

Statutory bodies, i.e. social services, health services, age concern and others, had enough faith in us to refer people to us – yet were unable to fund us. We raised money by running a charity shop, organising various fundraising activities and [running] a catering service. We begged and borrowed from anyone and everyone. Members themselves built the community kitchen, bit by bit, teaching each other do-it-yourself skills along the way. Even so, funding became a problem. Application forms were often too vague, full of long words and jargon, and extremely complicated.

Looking back now, I can see that we had taken on too much – our volunteers were burning out in their efforts to alleviate the suffering of so many. We had no time to build a strong infrastructure of support and funding. Only five weeks after receiving our award, Sophie – my granddaughter – died suddenly at the age of 11. She had been one of our most fervent activists; only six years old when we started, Sophie was champion for the needs of sick children and was involved in raising £22,000 for children before she died.

Gina
Holdsworth

We were the grassroots of the community, and yet there was no structure in place to support us through our most difficult time. The group couldn't survive and eventually closed its doors [in] June 2001.

During its time, it had helped develop 14 local groups, a local forum, 17 local activists, participation workers, three trainers, one development worker, one local community newspaper and, recently, one local councillor.

RISING UP AGAIN IN BRANSHOLME

Unlike many workers, we still live on Bransholme. The issues haven't gone away, [and] we have no option but to learn from our mistakes, use our knowledge, pick ourselves up, dust ourselves down and begin again.

Bransholme now has SRB6 [Single Regeneration Budget round 6] funding, which Motivation members worked hard to win. With this support, we intend to rise again, but plan this time to include:

- a firm structure and business plan

- core funding

- professional support

- a less diverse and more focused agenda

- first-hand experience.

Looking back, things that may have helped include:

- Hands-on support in navigating the procedure for charitable status. After two years of being told we did not qualify, we were told that actually we did. There [were] two further years when forms were lost and mislaid. The result was that we never did acquire charity status – something that many funders required.

- Funding application forms that are easy to read [and] complete.

- Partnerships that take into account the symptoms as well as the solutions – i.e. parenting forums offering crèches during meetings.

- Events/activities aimed at alleviating poverty, which include paying for expenses of those attending.

■ Councillors that actively encourage and support empowerment.

■ Recognition of the need and benefits of community support and development.

We ask if the following is possible:

■ An acknowledgement that there exists a difference between the grass and its roots.

■ The recognition that the label 'socially excluded' involves many complex issues that may often effect several generations.

■ That a flexible approach is developed, whereby training and support would be tailored to meet individuals' needs.

■ That community groups be given the funding and support required to engage with local residents – encouraging and building self-esteem, confidence and citizenship.

There have been times when I've looked at myself [as] just an ordinary housewife, but my kitchen is not only full of washing but also people and paperwork; and I look at people like Mary and Lesley, and I know that in their development, begins the development of our community.

Gina
Holdsworth

GEOFF MANFIELD
Community-led learning

> Community involvement is both an essential input and [a] desired outcome for any successful self-help project. Achieving this is perhaps the core problem of community development.
>
> **POLICY ACTION TEAM 9 – COMMUNITY SELF-HELP, 2000**

THE HAVERCROFT SKILLS PROJECT is one of a number of community-led learning centres across the Wakefield district. Geoff Manfield, who manages the centre, describes how it all started.

COMMUNITY EDUCATION IN ACTION – HOW IT ALL BEGAN

I was made redundant from Nostell pit in November 1987. There were many other pits round about which closed at the same time. I took advantage of some training in job search skills and CV writing at a resource centre in another village about eight miles from where I live. While I was on the course, I was asked if I wanted to join the management group of the centre. I soon realised that this type of provision was exactly what was needed in Havercroft. The village is in the middle of nowhere, between Wakefield and Barnsley, with infrequent bus services to both places. Havercroft and the adjoining villages of Ryhill and South Hiendley were badly affected by the pit closure programme, which had a devastating effect on the local community. It seemed as if everything went down in one go. I saw that learning was a way of refocusing and regenerating our community.

The opportunity came when the idea of outreach provision was raised, but even then it took a great deal of persistence and lobbying to get it to happen. At one time, it seemed as if there was every reason in the world for it not to. A group of us got together, and we were determined to make it succeed. We persuaded the local parish council to let us have the use of the local hall to run a ten-week pilot course in IT [information technology]. After that, there was no way we were going to give up. If we could show the demand was there, it would have to carry on.

We leafleted the local area with questionnaires and came up with the evidence. There were enough people interested to set up courses in computing, English and maths, video-making and sewing. Everything grew from there. Establishing a close relationship with the local authority's Adult Education Service began to give us access to the resources we needed. We soon became the biggest users of the parish hall and began to make alterations to the building.

At the same time, we were involved in other campaigns locally. For example, we led the campaign against British Coal's position of not letting their properties and of boarding houses up as soon as someone had moved out: the village was beginning to look like a war zone. We set a tenants and residents group up to persuade British Coal to reverse their decision, and when they sold the housing stock to a housing association based hundreds of miles away from Havercroft, we lobbied the community to sign up to changing to a local-based housing association. The houses were improved and are now fully occupied.

At the beginning, we were all volunteers and only got expenses – and sometimes barely that. I remember going on a visit to a centre in Middlesbrough and having to ask for a receipt for fish and chips – they wrote it on the chip paper!

The centre has now become well established, with over 700 learners a year. All the staff at the centre are paid the [going] rate for the job. We are very concerned about quality and make sure we get the tutors we want. We work closely with local people to make sure what we offer is what they want. We are still driven by our original aim, which is to get people jobs.

As a group, we have also made a successful lottery bid to build a sports hall and leisure centre on adjacent land, and just over two years ago, the parish hall was completely refurbished, so that we now have a brand new building which is entirely dedicated to learning.

Geoff
Mansfield

Conclusion

Neighbourhood Renewal–the Real Test

What is the real measure of the success of neighbourhood renewal initiatives? Is it 'hard outputs' – for example, the number of people who find jobs or take on new training opportunities? Is it 'soft outcomes' – for example, the number of people from traditionally non-participatory groups whose capacity is developed so they can participate in local decision-making? Is it about civic pride and active citizenship? Neighbourhood renewal is, of course, about all of these things and more, but the real issue is how these measures impact on communities to reduce poverty and improve quality of life for those with impoverished lives of poor quality.

The case studies show that, all over the country, committed individuals and organisations with a profound sense of social justice are involved in innovation, partnership, dedication and hard work. There are countless examples of individuals whose lives have been turned around – from upside-down and desperate to right-side up, productive and worthwhile. Likewise, community activists and adult and community learning tutors all over the country have experienced an immense sense of achievement as they watched learners grow and achieve everything they knew they could.

What the case studies do not – and cannot – show is how widespread this good practice is. Nor can they measure the impact over time of the various initiatives described – what's presented is a snapshot of nationwide good practice.

Most case studies acknowledge the importance of enabling people from poor communities to participate in activities that can have life-changing implications or, in some instances, in local strategic partnerships, Single Regeneration Budget partnerships, residents' associations and Community Forums. At the same time, the case studies recognise that partnerships are complicated to establish – particularly when people are coming together with different perspectives, experiences and interests. This is why many case studies allude to the thorny issues of lack of trust, confidence and belief in neighbourhood renewal.

The talking points that follow relate to neighbourhood renewal and form the conclusion to this book. They are intended to stimulate discussion about neighbourhood renewal.

TALKING POINTS

1 / Learning and neighbourhood renewal

The link between learning and neighbourhood renewal can often seem tenuous – particularly when new adult learners are accessing first-rung provision of learning that does not seem to contribute towards the regeneration of communities. However, initial building blocks can lead to greater challenges and levels of participation. The main assertion of this book is that there is no neighbourhood renewal without adult learning. Although not every learning adult will make an impact on their community, they have the potential to effect change in poor communities in ways not recognised in the past because of a 'top-down' approach.

In what ways can the impact of adult learning on neighbourhood renewal be measured?

Is it possible, for example, to devise a way of assessing the impact that adult learning can have on a community?

2 / The language of neighbourhood renewal

The phrases and language of neighbourhood renewal can often seem patronising, because they fail to recognise the significant achievements that people in ailing communities have made without mainstream interventions. Phrases such as 'deprived communities', 'poor people' and 'empowerment' can mask the fact that ailing communities often contain a dynamism and power that enables people to survive, and indeed prosper, against the odds.

How might people in such communities achieve a position from which they can define themselves in more appropriate ways?

3 / Conflict between community groups and mainstream institutions

A number of case studies show that, despite the fact the Government recognises that learning to make neighbourhood renewal work involves lessons for all partners, civil servants, Local Government, Councils of Voluntary Services, community groups and so on, tensions still can stifle development.

What suggestions do you have that might foster better relationships and greater levels of trust?

4 / Having the skills to do the job

Many initiatives in which organisations collaborate to produce a holistic approach to the problems of people in ailing communities demonstrate contradictions. A common contradiction is that those enlisted to manage such initiatives have little knowledge or understanding of the communities they are trying to help. Are there any short-terms solutions to this problem? Things to consider here might include:

- Positive action training, which is permissible under the Race Relations Act, Sexual Discrimination Act and Disability Discrimination Act.

- Community Leadership Programmes that allow identification of potential leaders and provide appropriate training.

- Fast track and work shadowing programmes that enable people in ailing communities to gain first-hand experience of the strategic and policy-orientated aspects of neighbourhood renewal.

■ Setting targets, which ensures that community members play a part, sometimes an employed part, in the regeneration of their communities.

5 / Measuring quality and impact in neighbourhood renewal

Measuring the effectiveness of a service can be difficult, especially when the service has no hard outputs such as accreditation. How can community capacity-building, empowerment and voluntary work be measured? Some indicators might be:

■ Better representation of people from excluded groups – particularly black people – on community forums, in residents' associations and so on.

■ More applications for jobs in the 'regeneration industry' from people from socially excluded groups.

■ Greater levels of participation at public meetings and consultation events.

■ Increased numbers of self-help, community-based organisations.

■ Increased viability of community groups and the services they deliver.

6 / Employment issues

A number of issues must be considered when relationships between employers, business and neighbourhood renewal are examined. The Neighbourhood Renewal Strategy emphasises the importance of the strategic role of businesses in developing communities – particularly in relation to encouraging investment. New opportunities require training and can lead to employment opportunities.

Are new employment opportunities always in the best interest of the community though? With regard to shops, one of Policy Action Team 13's key findings was that:

The majority of shops that traditionally served those living in deprived neighbourhoods were small, independent, convenience-type stores. While the number of superstores in this country has increased from 457 in 1986 to 1,102 by 1997, some eight independent shops disappeared every day between 1986 and 1996. For people on low income[s], shopping journeys by car and the average distance travelled to shops [have] increased.

A lack of competition from alternative convenience stores in local areas sometimes leads to overpricing, and the poorest and least mobile end up paying the most.

How do superstores – often multinationals – impact upon ailing communities? Some questions to consider:

■ Do local people work in new community-based shops and services?

■ Are they on a fair wage or salary?

Conclusion

147

■ Do employees have employment rights – like the right to join a union?

■ Does the employer provide training and promotional opportunities?

■ Is the new employer committed to neighbourhood renewal developments in the community?

7 / Putting the poorest people in the driver's seat

Several of the case studies are good examples of how the poorest people in our society can effectively be involved in decision-making about the future of their neighbourhoods. Unfortunately, however, the benefits system often gets in the way of such participation, because not being available for work can effect benefit claims. Are there any solutions to this?

Policy Action Team 9 – Self-help recommends that:

The Benefits Agency rules should be modified so that small advance payments by voluntary organisations made to cover volunteers' costs, such as travel expenses, do not effect benefits entitlements.

Are there any other ways in which the millions of hours spent in voluntary and community work can be recognised and rewarded appropriately? Some areas to consider would include:

■ Local exchange schemes through which services rather than money are exchanged.

■ Provision of travel warrants, meals and childcare.

■ Encouraging attendance at consultation and training events by providing record, book and mobile phone tokens or vouchers towards the purchase of computers, white goods and electrical equipment (but being aware of the sensitivities involved in providing vouchers, tokens and so on, which can seem 'tokenistic' and patronising).

Useful Reading & Websites

FURTHER READING

Lifelines Series, published by NIACE 2002:

Community Education and Neighbourhood Renewal, Jane Thompson, NIACE, 2002

Spreading the Word – Reaching Out to New Learners, Veronica McGivney, NIACE, 2002

Managing Community Projects for Change, Jan Eldred, NIACE, 2002

Engaging Black Learners in Adult and Community Education, Lenford White, NIACE, 2002

The Learning Curve – Developing Skills and Knowledge for Neighbourhood Renewal, Neighbourhood Renewal Unit October 2002.

Education for Critical Consciousness, Paulo Freire, Myra B. Ramos (Translator)

Pedagogy of the Oppressed, Paulo Freire, 1972

A New Commitment to Neighbourhood Renewal, National Strategy Action Plan. Neighbourhood Renewal Unit, 2001

Neighbourhood Renewal Unit Skills and Knowledge Programme – Helping People Improve Neighbourhoods, NRU, 2001

Report of Policy Action Team 16: Learning Lessons, NRU, 2000

Policy Action Team Report Summaries: A Compendium, NRU, 2000

Useful Websites:

www.dfes.gov.uk/index.htm Department for Education and Skills

http://www.neighbourhood.gov.uk/ Neighbourhood Renewal Unit

http://www.neighbourhood.gov.uk/publicationsdetail.asp?id=89 National Strategy for Neighbourhood Renewal

www.renewal.net 'Helping People Improve Neighbourhoods'

http://www.neighbourhood.gov.uk/nrfund.asp Neighbourhood Renewal Fund

http://www.neighbourhood.gov.uk/formatteddoc.asp?id=243 Neighbourhood Renewal Unit Research Strategy

http://www.neighbourhood.gov.uk/sandk.asp Neighbourhood Renewal Unit Skills and Knowledge

http://www.lsc.gov.uk/ Learning and Skills Council

http://www.whistleblower.nstemp.com/ Whistleblower Website

www.grantham.ac.uk & **www.yes4.co.uk** Grantham College

www.residentsonline.org.uk Residents Online

www.actionforhealth.freeserve.co.uk Action For Health

www.ydf.org.uk Yemeni Development foundation

www.niace.org.uk NIACE, National Institute of Adult continuing Education

www.fairbridge.org.uk Fairbridge

www.magpie123.org.uk Magpie Resource Library

http://www.cre.gov.uk/ Commission for Racial Equality

http://www.ncvo-vol.org.uk/ National Council for Voluntary Organisations.

http://www.info4local.gov.uk/ Information for Local Government

List of Contributors

This publication was supported by funding from the Department for Education and Skills.

MIKE LANE
37 Botanic Road, Liverpool L7 5PX
Tel: 07770 478756
Regeneration Watch
e: www.whistleblower.nstemp.com

ADULT COMMUNITY LEARNING
Sharon Gamble Training/Project
Co-ordinator
Willow
The North Hull Women's Centre
Hall Road Primary School
Hal Road
Hull HU6 8PP
tel: 01482 474094
e: sharon.gamble@hullcc.gov.uk

WAYNE NAYLOR
Braunstone Motor Project
Cantrell Road Centre
9 Cantrell Road
Braunstone
Leicester LE3 1SD
tel: 0116 2892186
e: BMPPROJ@aol.com

COMMUNITY LEADERSHIP
PROGRAMME
Machel Bogues
Bernie Grant Trust
266-268 High Road
Tottenham
London N15 4AJ
tel: 0208 880 9100

FLAGSHIP PROJECT
Susan Henley-Place MBE,
Mersey Heritage Trust Projects Office
11 Greenbank Drive
Sefton Park
Liverpool L17 1AN
tel: 0151 733 0699
e: merseyheritage@btinternet.com

FAIRBRIDGE SOLENT AND FUNKY
FURNITURE
Dawn Parker
The Orchard Centre
1 Orchard Lane
Southampton SO14 3BN
tel: 02380 231666
e: dparker@fairbridge.org.uk
w: www.fairbridge.org.uk

GRANTHAM COLLEGE - YES PROJECT
Tom Crowther
Grantham College
Stonebridge Road
Grantham
Lincs NG31 9AP
tel: 01476 400234
e: tcrowther@grantham.ac.uk
w: www.grantham.ac.uk and
www.yes4.co.uk

JET EASTERN LINK
Lynne Debbazi
Job Bank
4 Tunnel Road
Liverpool L7 6QD
tel: 0151 233 6118
e: lynne.debbazi@liverpool.gov.uk
w: www.jeteasternlink.co.uk

KEIGHLEY HEALTH LIVING
NETWORK
Jill Kibble
Action for Health
43-49 Lawkholme Lane
Keighley
Bradford BD21 3EA
tel: khln@actionforhealth.freeserve.co.uk
w: www.actionforhealth.freeserve.co.uk

L & Q RESIDENTS ONLINE
Maggie Gebbett
c/o London & Quadrant Housing Trust
Osborn House
Osborn Terrace
London SE3 9DR
tel: 0207 557 2014
e: mgebbett@lqgroup.org.uk
w: www.residentsonline.org.uk

LEARNING CHOICES
Caroline Tulett
Coquet House
Dr Thomlinson' C of E Middle School
Silverton Lane
Rothbury
Northumberland NE65 7RJ
tel: 01669 621899
e: learningchoices@supanet.com

LIVERPOOL CITY COUNCIL
COMMUNITY MATTERS
Training Unit (1991-2001)
Colin Watts
Community Roots to Success
KWUC
Kensington High Street
Liverpool L7 2RG
tel: 0151 222 3121
e: crts@supanet.com

MAGPIE RESOURCE LIBRARY
Encouraging Active Citizenship
441 New Cross Road
New Cross
London SE14 6TA
tel: 0208 692 7115
e: Magpie@441nx.org.uk
w: www.magpie123.org.uk

NORWICH LEARNING CITY:
DEVELOPING A COMMUNITY LED
APPROACH TO LEARNING
Chris Popplewell
Norwich City Council
City Hall
Norwich NR2 1WP
tel: 01603 212405
e: chrispopplewell@norwich.gov.uk

REDDITCH LOCAL LEARNING
CENTRE
Jenny Murray
Interact 21Ltd
The Granary
Brockhill Court, Brockhill Lane
Redditch B97 6RB
tel: 01527 588970
e: jenny.murray@interact21.com

YEMENI DEVELOPMENT
FOUNDATION
Mohammad Almasyabi
Magnolia House
73 Conybere Street
Highgate
Birmingham B12 0YL
tel: 0121 685 1800
e: admin@ydf.org.uk
w: www.ydf.org.uk

YES
Catherine Johnson
Grantham College
Stonebridge Road
Grantham
Links
tel: 01476 404375
e: cjohnson@grantham.ac.uk
w: www.yes4.co.uk